BREAKFAST OF CHAMPIONS

Kurt Vonnegut

3 1257 01809 5785

AUTHORED by Meghan Joyce
UPDATED AND REVISED by Damien Chazelle

COVER DESIGN by Table XI Partners LLC
COVER PHOTO by Olivia Verma and © 2005 GradeSaver, LLC

BOOK DESIGN by Table XI Partners LLC

Published by GradeSaver LLC, www.gradesaver.com

First published in the United States of America by GradeSaver LLC. 2008

GRADESAVER, the GradeSaver logo and the phrase "Getting you the grade since 1999" are registered trademarks of GradeSaver, LLC

ISBN 978-1-60259-164-6

Printed in the United States of America

For other products and additional information please visit
http://www.gradesaver.com

Table of Contents

Table of Contents

Biography of Vonnegut, Kurt (1922-2007)

One of the 20th century's great American pacifists was born on Armistice Day. Born in Indianapolis on November 11, 1922, Kurt Vonnegut entered a well-to-do family that was hit very hard by the Depression. Vonnegut went to public high school, unlike his two older siblings, and there gained early writing experience writing for the high school's daily paper. He enrolled at Cornell University in 1940 and, under pressure from his father and older brother, studied chemistry and biology. He had little real love for the subjects, and his performance was poor. He did, however, enjoy working for the *Cornell Daily Sun*. In 1942, Vonnegut left Cornell as the university was preparing to ask him to leave due to poor academic performance. He enrolled at the Carnegie Institute of Technology (now Carnegie-Mellon) in 1943. He studied there only briefly before enlisting in the U.S. Army. His mother killed herself by overdosing on sleeping pills in May 1944. In 1984, Vonnegut himself would attempt suicide by pills and alcohol.

On December 14, 1944, Vonnegut was captured in the Battle of the Bulge. He was held as a POW in Dresden, a beautiful German city with no major industries or military presence. The bombing of Dresden was unexpected. Vonnegut and the other POWs were some of the only survivors. They waited out the bombing in a meat cellar deep under the slaughterhouse.

Vonnegut was repatriated in May 1945. He returned to the United States and married Jane Marie Cox. He studied anthropology at the University of Chicago, but the department unanimously rejected his M.A. thesis. (According to the university's rules, a high-quality piece of writing could be substituted for a dissertation. Twenty years later, Vonnegut showed the department Cat's Cradle, and he was given his degree in 1971.) Vonnegut worked various jobs during his time at the University of Chicago and throughout the 1950s.

Vonnegut's first short story, "Report on the Barnhouse Effect," was published in 1950. Vonnegut has expressed some dissatisfaction with his short stories, saying that he mostly wrote them for money while working on his novels, which are more important to him. But some of his stories are accomplished works in their own right, and many readers gain their first exposure to Vonnegut through these stories, which combine in condensed form Vonnegut's trademark humor, fantasy, and social commentary. Dozens of Vonnegut's short stories and two novels appeared in the 1950s.

When his sister and her husband both died in 1958, Vonnegut adopted their three eldest children. He and his first wife had three children of their own, and they later adopted a seventh. Jane Marie Cox and Vonnegut separated in 1970, and in 1979 he married photographer Jill Krementz.

Due to his reputation as a science fiction writer, Vonnegut's first novels were published only as paperbacks with gaudy covers that misrepresented the novels and discouraged serious critical attention. The hardcover editions of Cat's Cradle (1963) and *God Bless You, Mr. Rosewater* (1965) were a significant improvement, although they sold only a few thousand copies. In 1966-1967, all of Vonnegut's novels were reissued in paperback, and he began to develop a significant underground following.

During the 1960s, Vonnegut published a collection of short stories and four more novels, including his sixth and greatest novel, Slaughterhouse Five. The novel's popularity and broad critical acclaim focused new attention on Vonnegut's earlier work, and soon *The Sirens of Titan* sold over 200,000 copies.

He has continued to write prolifically. His most recent novel is *Timequake* (1997). With its publication, he retired from fiction writing. His most recent book of essays is *A Man without a Country* (2005). He worked as a senior editor at *In These Times*, a progressive Chicago magazine, until his death.

Vonnegut has been an important mentor for young pacifists since he began writing. His novels are known for their dark humor and playful use of science fiction, as well as their serious moral vision and cutting social commentary. Although his novels have been criticized for being too simplistic, he has a cult following of readers who love his imagination and sense of humor. He is at once irreverent and highly moral, and this rare combination has made his voice integral to American literature.

Kurt Vonnegut passed away in 2007.

About Breakfast of Champions

Published in 1973, *Breakfast of Champions* or *Goodbye, Blue Monday!* was Kurt Vonnegut's 50th birthday present to himself. It also marked the end of a period of depression that had followed his 1969 publication of *Slaughterhouse Five*.

The alternate title might have come from George Gershwin and Buddy DeSylva's 1922 one-act opera, *Blue Monday*, later renamed [135th Street.] This twenty- to thirty-minute work was written for an all-black cast, but was performed by white actors in blackface - a salient fact considering the theme of race that pervades *Breakfast of Champions*. The narrator of *Breakfast of Champions* always distinguishes the race of each character, and the potential reference to the opera would also imply that the phrase *Goodbye, Blue Monday* has some meaning as a symbol - as opposed to the suggestion at the end of Vonnegut's tale that symbols are mere constructs of the American mind.

Breakfast of Champions tells the story of Kilgore Trout, an elderly science fiction author and one of Vonnegut's recurring characters, and Dwayne Hoover, an insane but wealthy Pontiac dealer who interprets Trout's work literally. When the two finally meet in a bar, Hoover becomes violent, attacking bystanders and biting off Trout's finger.

Vonnegut experiments with structure, most obviously when it comes to the inclusion of his own child-like sketches. The sketches are used to demonstrate the use of symbols, which the narrator depends upon heavily and then dismisses, in the Epilogue, as an unnecessary American tendency. For example, there are two drawings of an apple throughout the story; in the Epilogue, when the narrator holds out his empty hands to Kilgore Trout and asks him what he sees in them, Trout sees an apple. The apple is a common American symbol, and demonstrates the narrator's point that Americans depend upon the meaning in symbols.

A 1999 film version of *Breakfast of Champions* stars Bruce Willis as Dwayne Hoover and Albert Finney as Kilgore Trout. It was adapted and directed by Alan Rudolph.

Character List

Abe Cohen

The jeweler in the cocktail lounge of the new Holiday Inn. When he sees Mary Alice Miller walk through, he despises her "sexlessness and innocence and empty mind" and says, "Pure tuna fish!"

Andy Lieber

The driver of the Ford *Galaxie* in which Kilgore Trout hitchhikes. He is a thirty-two year old, white, overweight traveling salesman, "obviously a happy man" and a crazy driver. He has averaged twenty-two orgasms per month over the past year, "far above the national average."

Bill

Bill is Kilgore Trout's parakeet. Trout thinks that Bill will die a few moments before he does, and confides in Bill that humanity deserves to die horribly.

In Chapter 3, there is an important interaction between Trout and Bill, in which Trout opens the parakeet's cage so Bill can fly to the window. Bill puts his shoulder against the glass, but when Trout opens the window, Bill is scared and flies back into his cage.

Beatrice Keedsler

The Gothic novelist who attends the arts festival in Midland City. In Chapter 18, she is introduced as she enters the new Holiday Inn cocktail lounge with Rabo Karabekian. She grew up in Midland City, and says she was "petrified of coming home after all these years."

Dwayne Hoover breaks her jaw during his rampage.

Bonnie MacMahon

The white cocktail waitress who serves Dwayne Hoover at the new Holiday Inn cocktail lounge. They are longtime acquaintances, and they have bought nine Pontiacs from him over the past sixteen years. Bonnie makes the same joke every time she serves a customer a martini: "Breakfast of Champions." She wears "octagonal, rimless trifocals," and is "a horse-faced woman forty-two years old."

Her two goals in life are to earn back all the money her husband lost by investing in a car wash, and to get steel-belted radial tires for the front wheels of her car.

The narrator offers to tell her fortune, but she refuses. He reveals to the reader that her fortune is:

You will be swindled by termite exterminators and not even
know it. You will buy steel-belted radial tires for teh front
wheels of your car. Your cat will be killd by a motorcyclist
named Headley Thomas, and you will get another car. Arthur,
your brother in Atlanta, will find eleven dollars in a taxicab.

The inclusion of these details in her fortune foreshadows the idea that is explained
later in Chapter 19, that no detail is more important than any other.

Bunny Hoover

Dwayne Hoover's homosexual son, who plays the piano in the cocktail lounge of
the new Holiday Inn. His real name is George. He only eats raw fruits and
vegetables, avoids the sunshine, and has no "friends or lovers or pets." He lives on
Skid Row, and his window looks out to the old Opera House. He practices
Transcendental Meditation, which he learned from Maharishi Mahesh Yogi. It
allows him to remove himself mentally while he is playing the piano. When he
told his father he wished he were a woman, he was sent away to military school
when he was only 10 years old. There he had "eight years of uninterrupted sports,
buggery and Fascism."

The narrator reveals that his fortune is:

Your father will become extremely ill, and you will respond so
grotesquely that there will be talk of putting you in the booby
hatch, too. You will stage scenes in the hospital waiting room,
telling doctors and nurses that you are to blame for your father's
disease. You will blame yourself for trying for so many years to
kill him with hatred. You will redirect your hatred. You will hate
your mom.

This is the only instance in which Bunny's future, beyond the realm of the story, is
revealed to the reader.

During his rampage, Dwayne Hoover, his father, slams his head again and again
onto the piano keys, leaving his face unrecognizable "even as a face - anybody's
face."

Celia Hoover

Dwayne's wife, who has committed suicide by eating Drano. The description of
her death uses the theme of humans as machines: "Celia became a small volcano,
since she was composed of the same sorts of substances which commonly clogged
drains."

She is likened to the narrator's mother in Chapter 16, because both are "crazy as a
bedbug," "beautiful in exotic ways," and both committed suicide. Also, neither

woman could stand to have her picture taken.

Cyprian Ukwende

The black intern at the County Hospital. He earned a medical degree at Harvard and has been in Midland City for a week. He is an Indaro, a Nigerian, an identity trait that is emphasized each time he is mentioned in the story. He is pointedly different from American blacks, since his relatives were not slaves and he feels "kinship only with Indaros."

We are first introduced to him in Chapter 6, because he is the only person with Mary Young while she dies. He is staying in the new Holiday Inn, owned in part by Dwayne Hoover, until he can find a cheap apartment in which to live. He also needs a woman, because he is "so full of lust and jism all the time." In Chapter 11 we learn that though he appears impassive, "behind his mask was a young man in the terminal stages of nostalgia and lover's nuts."

Delmore Skag

A character in one of Trout's novels. He is a scientist who discovers a way to reproduce himself by mixing cells from his right hand with chicken soup. He hoped to "force his country into making laws against excessively large families," but instead, after he fathers hundreds and hundreds of children, America passes laws against "possession by unmarried persons of chicken soup."

Don Breedlove

A gas-conversion unit installer, and the only person whom Dwayne hurt who deserved it, according to the narrator. He raped Patty Keene in the parking lot of George Hickman Bannister Memorial Fieldhouse.

Dwayne once sold him a Pontiac *Ventura*, and had made adjustments and replaced parts because it wouldn't run right. But Breedlove had painted, "This Car is a Lemon" all over the car. It turned out a neighborhood kid had poured maple syrup in its gas tank.

He had been repairing a defective gas oven in the kitchen of the new Holiday Inn during Dwayne's rampage. Dwayne offers Breedlove his hand, and they shake; while Breedlove is led to believe Dwayne is making a motion of friendship, Dwayne boxes him in the ear, causing him to go deaf.

Don Miller

Mary Alice Miller's father, who taught her to swim when she was eight months old and forced her to swim for at least four hours every day since the age of three. At the time Dwayne Hoover bursts outside after attacking three people in the new Holiday Inn cocktail lounge, Don Miller is lying in his car with the seat back flat, learning French on audio tape.

Dwayne Hoover

A "fabulously well-to-do" Pontiac dealer, Hoover is also a "novice lunatic." A combination of drug abuse and powerful ideas has brought him to the brink of madness. He reads Trout's science-fiction and interprets it literally, believing that everyone else in the world is a robot.

Dwayne was adopted, and his birth parents are described as machines in Chapter 3: "Dwayne's real mother was a spinster school teacher who wrote sentimental poetry and claimed to be descended from Richard the Lion-Hearted, who was a king. His real father was an itinerant typesetter... She was defective child-bearing machine. She destroyed herself automatically while giving birth to Dwayne. The printer disappeared. He was a disappearing machine." It is important to note that both Dwayne's birth mother and his adoptive mother are described as destroying themselves, one in childbirth and the other with pills. The speaker's mother killed herself, as well.

We find out in Chapter 13 that he was adopted by people who thought they couldn't have children, but who later *did* give birth to the twins Lyle and Kyle.

Eddie Key

The driver of *The Martha Simmons Memorial Mobile Disaster Unit* when it picks up Dwayne Hoover and his victims. He is a young, black, direct descendant of Francis Scott Key, and knows all about his personal ancestry as he was the chosen member of his generation to memorize the family history.

He can be seen as representing the history of America as it interacts with the future, including all races since his ancestors are white, black, and "Indians." As he drives the emergency vehicle, he has "the feeling that he himself was a vehicle, and that his eyes were windshields through which his progenitors could look, if they wished to." In case Francis Scott Key is looking through at what has become of America, Eddie focuses his eyes on the American flag stuck to the windshield and murmurs, "Still wavin', man."

Eldon Robbins

A black male dishwasher at the new Holiday Inn cocktail lounge. He recognizes Wayne Hoobler outside near the trashcans, because he too has spent time in the Adult Correctional Institution. He brings Wayne inside, gives him a meal, and shows him the peephole through which the black dishwashers watch the white customers in the cocktail lounge.

Eliot Rosewater

The eccentric millionaire who spent $18,000 tracking down Trout so he can send him a fan letter. He leverages his El Greco painting in an agreement with Fred T. Barry, to ensure that Trout will be invited to the arts festival.

He accidentally killed his mother in a boating accident when he was young. The narrator tells us, "I made Rosewater an alcoholic in another book," but now he is sobered up thanks to Alcoholics Anonymous. He has been having orgies with strangers in New York City.

Francine Pefko

Dwayne's secretary and mistress. She is described in Chapter 13 as "a war widow with lips like sofa pillows and bright red hair," and in Chapter 15 as a "generous, voluptuous woman." She is in love with Dwayne, and tells him so in Chapter 15 even though they have made a pact not to speak about love.

Her husband, Robert Pefko, died in Viet Nam. She had followed him to Midland City, where he worked on the manufacture of a new "booby trap" to be used in the military.

Fred T. Barry

The chairman of the arts festival in Midland City, who sends the invitation to Kilgore Trout. The two men are exactly the same age. As Fred T. Barry grew older and happier, he came to resemble "an ecstatic old Chinaman" more and more. He even starts dressing like a Chinaman.

Gloria Browning

The white cashier in the Service Department, who covers "The Nerve Center" (Francine Pefko's desk) while Francine escapes to have sex with Dwayne Hoover. She is twenty-five and has just had a hysterectomy after a botched abortion. The father of the "destroyed fetus" was Don Breedlove, the same man who had raped Patty Keene.

Harold Newcomb Wilbur

The bartender in the new Holiday Inn cocktail lounge. He is the second most decorated veteran in Midland City. When he stares at the narrator, the narrator decides to have him receive a phone call from Ned Lingamon in prison.

Harry LeSabre

Dwayne's sales manager at the Pontiac agency. He is the first person to notice Dwayne's strange behavior. He is also a closeted transvestite, and worries that Dwayne knows his secret because of implications he invents in Dwayne's meaningless rants.

He is well-to-do because he invested wisely in the stock market, specifically in Xerox. He and his wife Grace move to Maui after he erroneously worries that he will be fired for being discovered as a transvestite.

Kazak

The Doberman pinscher that attacks the narrator in the Epilogue. He has been taught that "the Creator of the Universe wanted him to kill anything he could catch, and eat it, too." Ironically, he ends up attacking the Creator of the Universe, the narrator, as he loiters in front of the fence behind which the dog is kept.

Khashdrahr Miasma

Cyprian Ukwende's Bengali assistant, who is unhelpful on *Martha*. He refuses to find shears to cut off Dwayne Hoover's shoes, which are coated in plastic from Sugar Creek. He cannot tolerate criticism, and he has just been criticized for amputating a black man's foot when the foot probably could have been saved.

Kilgore Trout

Trout is a science-fiction writer, a "nobody" who owns "doodley-squat." He feels as if he has no impact on the world, and is introduced in Chapter 1 as supposing, or hoping, he is dead. He works as an installer of aluminum combination storm windows and screens, and at first nobody knows he is a writer. He is described in Chapter 2 as having no charm.

He will win the Nobel Prize for Medicine in 1979.

Trout has been married three times, as we find out in his Chapter 12 conversation with the Pyramid truck driver. Each of his wifes had been "extraordinarily patient and loving and beautiful. Each had been shriveled by his pessimism." He also has only one son, who left home at the age of 14, and from whom Trout has never heard again. Trout does know that he deserted in Viet Nam and joined the Viet Cong.

The narrator tells us that, "Trout was the only character I ever created who had enough imagination to suspect that he might be the creation of another human being."

Lottie Davis

Dwayne's black servant. She was descended from slaves. She and Dwayne like each other, but they don't talk much.

Lyle and Kyle Hoover

Dwayne Hoover's younger stepbrothers who own Sacred Miracle Cave. They live in identical yellow ranch houses on either side of the gift shop. The only difference in their appearances is that Lyle had his nose broken at the Roller Derby in 1954.

They are exceedingly worried about the fate of the Sacred Miracle Cave, since stinky bubbles the size of ping-pong balls have been floating up from the polluted stream that runs through it.

Mary Alice Miller

The fifteen-year-old Women's Two Hundred Meter Breast Stroke Champion of the World. She is the only internationally famous person in Midland City, and is the Queen of the Festival of the Arts. Her father taught her to swim when she was eight months old, and made her swim at least four hours every day since she was three. When Bonnie MacMahon tells Robo Karabekian Mary Alice's story, he insults her and causes the spiritual climax of the book.

Her eyes are permanently inflamed, and her father, Don Miller, is Chairman of the Parole Board at Shepherdstown.

The manager

The manager of the pornographic movie house in Chapters 7 and 8 is also the ticket-taker, bouncer, and janitor. He is attacked by what comes to be known as *The Pluto Gang* along with Kilgore Trout on Forty-second Street. He says "God bless you" when Trout happens to sneeze, and they form a temporary friendship that lasts until they are attacked. He has a wife and two kids who don't know that he runs a pornographic theater. He was in on the development of "a miraculous insulating material," which is the same material of which Dwayne Hoover's house is made.

Mary Young

The oldest inhabitant of Midland City, who is dying in the County Hospital in Chapter 6. Her parents had been slaves in Kentucky. She is black, and she used to do the laundry for Dwayne's family. The only person with her while she dies is Cyprian Ukwende.

Milo Maritimo

The beautiful young desk clerk at the new Holiday Inn, and also the homosexual grandson of Guillermo "Little Willie" Maritimo, a "bodyguard of the notorious Chicago gangster, Al Capone. He is also the nephew of the partners in the Maritimo Brothers Construction Company, which is polluting Sugar Creek.

He has read all of Kilgore Trout's work, which he borrowed from the personal library of Eliot Rosewater, and gives Trout a surprisingly welcome greeting upon his arrival to the hotel.

The Narrator

The narrator inserts himself into the story. He discusses how he invented each of the characters, and how he is constantly deciding what happens to them.

He suspects that he has schizophrenia, although he is not certain. What he does know is that, "I was making myself hideously uncomfortable by not narrowing my attention to details of life which were immediately important, and by refusing to believe what my neighbors believed." This vague description is perhaps provided by Vonnegut in order to point to the more obvious symptom the narrator exhibits: interacting with characters in a fictional universe.

Ned Lingamon

The most decorated veteran in Midland City. He calls Harold Newcomb Wilbur from prison, where he is because he killed his own baby. His dead baby's name was Cynthia Anne, and he killed her because she wouldn't stop crying.

Newbolt Simmons

A County Commissioner of Public Safety, after whose wife the *Martha Simmons Memorial Mobile Disaster Unit* is named. His wife died of rabies after being bitten by a bat she was trying to save. He and Dwayne were "drawn together for a while," because their wifes had died strange deaths within a month of each other. Their friendship petered out, but they still exchange Christmas cards.

Patty Keene

Dwayne's waitress at the Burger Chef in Chapter 15, who believes she can convince Dwayne to help her financially. She is a seventeen-year-old white girl, with blond hair and blue eyes, working to pay off the hospital bills accrued by her father as he died of colon cancer.

She was raped by Don Breedlove, but never reported it to the police because she was preoccupied with her father's illness at the time.

Phoebe Hurty

In the Preface, Vonnegut dedicates *Breakfast of Champions* to Phoebe Hurty. She is impolite in a graceful way, a quality which Vonnegut says he tries to imitate. She represents the belief in a new American paradise that would come with prosperity after the Great Depression.

The Pyramid truck driver

The driver of the Pyramid truck that picks up Trout at the mouth of the Lincoln tunnel. His interactions with Trout point to themes of the story, such as his opinion about the destruction of the planet. His brother works in a factory making chemicals for killing plants and trees in Viet Nam. The driver points out that "the only kind of job an American can get these days is committing suicide in some way," meaning that most jobs destroy the planet, and consequently humankind.

Rabo Karabekian

The minimal painter who attends the arts festival in Midland City. His painting, entitled *The Temptation of Saint Anthony*, was the first purchase for the permanent collection of the Mildred Barry Memorial Center for the Arts, and cost $50,000.

He is, in the narrator's opinion, "a vain and weak and trashy man." This is perhaps because his opinion that all living things are beams of light, expressed in his painting, is so contrary to the narrator's conviction that humans are machines.

Sparky

Sparky is Dwayne Hoover's Labrador retriever. Because of a car accident in the past, he cannot wag his tail. Unfortunately, this means other dogs don't know how friendly he is, and he has to fight all the time.

Vernon Garr

A white mechanic at Dwayne's Pontiac agency. His wife, Mary, is a schizophrenic who believes that Vernon is trying to turn her brains into plutonium. Dwayne's previously philanthropic nature is exemplified in a conversation he had with Vernon, in which he shows concern for Vernon's wife's health.

Wayne Hoobler

Wayne Hoobler is introduced in Chapter 11. He has just been paroled from the Adult Correctional Institution at Shepherdstown, and feels as though he's free for the first time in his life, since he has always been kept in "orphanages and youth shelters and prisons of one sort or another." He believes that the planet is terrible, and feels like he doesn't belong on it since he has no friends or relatives, and is always being put in cages.

He comes looking for Dwayne Hoover because he has seen advertisements for the Pontiac dealership and he wants to work there. His idea of an ideal world is called Fairyland, a place he sees in his dreams. The speaker points out how *childish* the name is. He believes that working for Dwayne will help him achieve that Fairyland.

He misses prison, since now that he is free he doesn't know what to do with himself. This is similar to what happened to Bill, Trout's bird, when he freed it from its cage and it decided to hop back inside because it was afraid of what was beyond the window. This connection builds upon the theme of race, with black people being viewed as animals thanks to the society in which they have been brought up.

Wayne also has excellent, white teeth, thanks to the superb dental program available to prisoners at the Adult Correctional Institution at Shepherdstown.

Major Themes

Humans as Machines

Vonnegut introduces this theme in the Preface, saying the concept stems from his observation as a boy of men suffering from locomotor ataxia. It dictates the narrator's control over the characters in his created universe in this way:

> I could only guide their movements approximately, since they were such big animals. There was inertia to overcome. It wasn't as though I was connected to them by steel wires. It was more as though I was connected to them by stale rubberbands.

In fact, the narrator is not able to control actual machines in his own created universe any more than he is able to control the machine-characters. In the Epilogue, as he accosts Kilgore Trout, he struggles with the windshield wipers and cigarette lighter of the car he is driving as he tries to turn on the dome light and let Trout see him.

The narrator does not come to a conclusion about humans as machines until Chapter 19, when he decides, "There was nothing sacred about myself or about any human being, that we were all machines, doomed to collide and collide and collide."

In the first chapter, this theme carries an evil connotation, as thinking of human beings as machines was used to justify slavery and racism. The conquistadors of the new world, to whom Vonnegut refers as "pirates," used guns to "wreck the wiring or the bellows or the plumbing of a stubborn human being, even when he was far, far away."

This theme also has relevance in terms of Hoover's insanity: his problem is that he is convinced "everyone on Earth was a robot, with one exception - Dwayne Hoover." It is used to justify war in Chapter 19, when Harold Newcomb Wilbur is described as having earned his medals:

> [The] Second World War [...] was staged by robots so that Dwayne Hoover could give a free-willed reaction to such a holocaust. The war was such an extravaganza that there was scarcely a robot anywhere who didn't have a part to play. Harold Newcomb Wilbur got his medals for killing Japanese, who were yellow robots. They were fueled by rice.

This description enforces the idea that eventually overcomes Dwayne Hoover, presented to him in Trout's novel *Now It Can Be Told*. After reading it, in fact, Dwayne uses the idea of humans as machines to justify attacking everyone, since they cannot feel. When he rants to Wayne Hoobler outside in the parking lot, he concludes that nothing is really a shame, since "Why should I care what happens to machines?" This rationale could be used to justify any type of injustice.

The description of the humans in West Virgina furthers this characterization. The driver of the Pyramid truck tells Trout how he observed them going "around and around," unsmiling. This behavior is very much like a machine, especially since they were on wheels.

In Chapter 15, the people of Midland City are excused for not realizing that Dwayne Hoover was insane because of their machine-like qualities:

> Their imaginations insisted that nobody changed much from day to day. Their imaginations were flywheels on the ramshackle machinery of the awful truth.

This description is particularly important because it likens not only the human body to a machine, but the *mind*, which is often seen as the most distinctive quality of humans.

Dwayne Hoover likens himself to a machine, specifically a car, when he confides in Francine about his visit to the Pontiac Division of General Motors. He saw the "destructive testing" room, and couldn't help wondering if God had put him on Earth just to "find out how much a man could take without breaking."

Francine is later described as a machine herself, in Chapter 18 when she returns to work in the Pontiac agency: "Francine was pure machinery at the moment, a machine made of meat - a typing machine, a filing machine."

Emotional State of American Citizens

In the first chapter, the United States is introduced as important because it is the country in which Hoover and Trout live. Its citizens are described as "so ignored and cheated and insulted that they thought they might be in the wrong country, or even on the wrong planet, that some terrible mistake had been made." Vonnegut cites the national anthem, which is "gibberish sprinkled with question marks," the law against flag-dipping, and the motto "E pluribus unum" as factors that exacerbate the "nonsense" that makes America unique.

This disenchantment is explored in the character of the Pyramid truck driver, who posits that "the only kind of job an American can get these days is committing suicide in some way." He comes to this conclusion since his own job causes pollution and requires roads to be built; in this way, the destruction of the planet is inextricably linked to the destruction of humankind. And since we are the ones destroying the planet, we are destroying ourselves.

In Chapter 19, the narrator decides he finally understands what is plaguing

American citizens: "They were doing their best to live like people invented in story books." This revelation is possibly the opinion of Vonnegut as well as of his narrator. He notes:

> This was the reason Americans shot each other so often: It was a convenient literary device for ending short stories and books.

> Why were so many Americans treated by their government as though their lives were as disposable as paper facial tissues? Because that was the way authors customarily treated bit-part players in their made-up tales.

Ideas as Disease

"Ideas or the lack of them can cause disease!" This is what Trout proclaims when he realizes what his ideas have done to Hoover. He "became a fanatic on the importance of ideas as causes and cures for diseases." Trout's story *Plague on Wheels*, first described in Chapter 2, expresses the idea that "human beings could be as easily felled by single idea as by cholera or the bubonic plague." In this case, it is the idea of the automobile that destroys them. This theme is further developed in Chapter 8, when Trout's account of what happened the night he was attacked on Forty-second Street leads to the fabrication of *The Pluto Gang*. "His comment turned out to be the first germ in an epidemic of mind-poisoning."

Mirrors

Trout calls mirrors "leaks," because it amuses him "to pretend that mirrors were holes between two universes." In Chapter 10, he tells the driver of the Pyramid truck that where he comes from in Bermuda, mirrors are called leaks. The driver then tells his wife, and she tells her friends. In this way, the mirror=leak idea is used to demonstrate another theme, that of ideas spreading like disease.

The theme of mirrors is addressed in terms of Sugar Creek, "the only significant surface water within eight miles of Midland City." In Chapter 11, we learn that it floods sometimes, forming "a vast mirror in which children might safely play." This mirror acts as a leak in the sense that Kilgore Trout understands it, as a hole between the universe of the book and that of the speaker/author:

> The mirror showed the citizens the shape of the valley they lived in, demonstrated that they were hill people who inhabited slopes rising one inch for every mile that separated them from Sugar Creek.

The inhabitants are able to look into the mirror/leak and see themselves through the eyes of an observer.

In Chapter 18, when the narrator interacts with his characters in his created universe in the new Holiday Inn cocktail lounge, he tells us the readers that he is wearing sunglasses so that he can be incognito. His sunglasses likewise embody the idea of mirrors as "leaks":

> The lenses were silvered, were mirrors to anyone looking my way. Anyone wanting to know what my eyes were like was confronted with his or her own twin reflections. Where other people in the cocktail lounge had eyes, I had two holes into another universe. I had leaks.

Now the reader understands the purpose of Trout's calling mirrors "leaks" throughout the story. The narrator's sunglasses are truly leaks between universes: his own and that of the characters. He is able to watch his characters through the "leaks," but to the characters in their universe they are merely mirrors.

In Chapter 20, when Kilgore Trout arrives at the new Holiday Inn, he finds himself surrounded by "leaks" in the lobby: "And when Trout looked through them to see what was going on in the other universe, he saw a red-eyed, filthy old creature who was barefoot, who had his pants rolled up to his knees." Trout seems to be able to actually use the mirrors as "leaks," seeing himself as the narrator sees him.

In the Epilogue, as the narrator leaves the universe of his characters and, presumably, travels through the "void" back to his own universe, a small hand mirror floats by him. This literal mirror accompanies the "leak" it has represented throughout the whole story: the gap between universes through which the narrator now travels.

Tombstones

There are sketches of tombstones throughout the book. This suggests that humans will be "gone but not forgotten," as stated by Kago in Trout's story *Plague on Wheels*.

The first tombstone is that of Kilgore Trout, at the end of Chapter 1. It is actually a monument constructed in his honor by the American Academy of Arts and Sciences. It reads: "We are healthy only to the extent that our ideas are humane." The words are a quotation from his last novel, which was unfinished.

In Chapter 16, we learn the story of *Now It Can Be Told*, Trout's novel and a book that will drive Hoover crazy once and for all. In it, The Man (the experimental creature with free will) has a tombstone. The Man's tombstone reads: "Not Even The Creator of the Universe Knew What The Man Was Going to Say Next. Perhaps The Man Was a Better Universe in its Infancy."

In Chapter 18, the narrator suggests a tombstone for Wayne Hoobler, which reads: "Black Jailbird. He Adapted to What There Was to Adapt to." This tombstone message hints at the theme of race, since we usually think of animals as adapting to their environments. Black people throughout the story have been compared to animals, and here Wayne Hoobler's entire existence is summed up as one of adaptation. He misses what he knows, even though it is captivity, much as an animal would. In fact, this passage links him to Trout's bird Bill, who flew back into his cage because he was afraid of everything outside the window.

Ownership

This theme is important because Dwayne Hoover owns almost all of Midland City, including the new Holiday Inn where he snaps and begins hurting people.

The speaker seems to have a skeptical view of the idea of humans owning land, and this opinion is demonstrated in Trout's story "This Means You," in Chapter 8. In the story, all the land of the Hawaiian Islands is owned by about forty people, and they don't allow any trespassers. So all the other people who live there are forced to dangle from the strings of helium balloons, in order to obey the *No Trespassing* signs. This story is a hyperbole, in that it is unlikely this level of ownership and enforcement will ever occur, but it draws attention to the real problem at hand of some people (like Dwayne Hoover) owning everything, and others (like freed black slaves) owning nothing.

The problem of freed black slaves owning nothing is referenced directly in Chapter 8, in the form of the ancestors of the young black prostitutes, who were forced to come to cities because of *No Trespassing* signs everywhere else. It is again addressed in Chapter 10 when Trout catches a ride on the truck at the mouth of the Lincoln Tunnel: "The slaves were simply turned loose without any property. They were easily recognizable. They were black. They were suddenly free to go exploring." But from the tone of the rest of the book, we know the slaves' exploring didn't get them very far, and their lack of property was extremely hindering.

In Chapter 12, we are told of how Kilgore Trout once encountered the Governor of New York, Nelson Rockefeller, and didn't recognize him. The speaker takes this opportunity to demonstrate his cynicism about the rules of ownership, by noting that:

> Because of the peculiar laws in that part of the planet,
> Rockefeller was allowed to own vast areas of Earth's surface,
> and the petroleum and other valuable minerals underneath the
> surface, as well. He owned or controlled more of the planet than
> many nations. This had been his destiny since infancy. He had
> been *born* into that cockamamie proprietorship.

Another symbol of ownership is the old miner whom Trout encounters in West Virginia. He represents the feelings of a lot of Americans, saying that it "don't matter if you care if you don't own what you care about." The land he worked on was owned by Eliot Rosewater's company. The old miner tells Trout:

> "It don't seem right that a man can own what's underneath another man's farm or woods or house. And any time the man wants to get what's underneath all that, he's got a right to wreck what's on top to get at it. The rights of the people on top of the ground don't amount to nothing compared to the rights of the man who owns what's underneath."

The Destruction of the Planet

This theme is addressed in Chapter 10, when the truck driver points out that "The planet was being destroyed by manufacturing processes, and what was being manufactured was lousy, by and large."

The underground stream that passes through the Sacred Miracle Cave owned by Lyle and Kyle Hoover is polluted, and the bubbles smell like athlete's foot. This detail links the pollution of the stream under Sacred Miracle Cave to the disease that killed off the Ern in Bermuda. Pollution by humans not only destroyed the species of bird, it is destroying a tourist trap created by humans for humans.

West Virgina, as described in Chapter 14 as Trout passes through it with the driver of the Pyramid truck, can be seen as representing the greater problem of the destruction of the planet. Its surface "had been demolished by men and machinery and explosives in order to make it yield up its coal." Now, "with its coal and trees and topsoil gone, it was rearranging what was left of itself in conformity with the laws of gravity. It was collapsing into all the holes which had been dug into it." The speaker makes sure to point out that:

> The demolition of West Virginia had taken place with the approval of the executive, legislative, and judicial branches of the State Government, which drew their power from the people.

Thus, the blame lies on everyone.

Communisim

Communism is introduced in Chapter 1, with relation to "the wrecked planet" Earth. America's opinion of Communists is important:

> Dwayne Hoover's and Kilgore Trout's country, where there was still plenty of everything, was opposed to Communism. It didn't think that Earthlings who had a lot should sare it with others unless they really wanted to, and most of them didn't want to. So

they didn't have to.

In this way, the theme of anti-Communism is linked to the theme of ownership: some people, like Dwayne Hoover in the beginning of the story, are "fabulously well-to-do," while others have "doodley-squat."

This theme is addressed again in Trout's conversation with the Pyramid truck driver in Chapter 10. The driver's brother works in a factory that makes chemicals to kill foliage in Viet Nam, "a country where America was trying to make people stop being communists by dropping things on them from airplanes." By killing the plants and trees, the driver's brother is killing a source of life on the planet, and thus indirectly committing suicide. The fight against Communism proves a self-destructive one.

Advertising

In Chapter 4, Dwayne Hoover notices the advertisements on the radio in his car after he has stopped his crazed ride. He hears an advertisement for "ten different kinds of flowering shrubs and five fruit trees for six dollars, C.O.D." It sounds good to him, because he is susceptible to the charms of advertising, like a child. The speaker notes that:

> Almost all the messages which were sent and received in his
> country, even the telepathic ones, had to do with buying or
> selling some damn thing. They were like lullabies to Dwayne.

The diction choice of "lullabies" is significant, since it draws attention to the childlike quality necessary to be so moved by advertisements.

This theme is introduced again when Trout notices the word "PYRAMID" on the side of the truck he's been riding in in Chapter 10. He wonders "what a child who was just learning to read would make of a message like that," and decides that the child would think it was "terrifically important" since it is so big. In Chapter 12, Trout asks the Pyramid truck driver why the company is called *Pyramid*, since the truck is meant to transport things rapidly and pyramids don't move. The driver responds that his brother-in-law, who started the company, "liked the *sound* of it. Don't you like the *sound* of it?" Trout agrees just "to keep things friendly," then creates a little story in his head. It is about a planet where the creatures were so "enchanted by sounds" that the language kept turning into music. This was a problem since the music was useless as a conveyor of information, so the leaders had to keep inventing "new and much uglier vocabularies and sentence structures all the time, which would resist being transmuted to music." Thus, Trout harkens back to the advertisements "like lullabyes" in Chapter 4.

Wayne Hoobler banks his only hope in his new free life - to work for Dwayne Hoover at the Pontiac dealership - on an advertisement he's seen. He further links susceptibility to advertising to childishness: his whole existence in the story is based upon advertising, and his ideal world is called Fairyland, a word which the speaker points out is "childish." From the information he gathers from the advertisement, Wayne Hoobler believes that working for Dwayne will help him reach this quixotic destination.

In Chapter 16, Trout asks the driver of the *Galaxie* why he thinks a fire extinguisher brand would be named *Excelsior*, and the driver shrugs and answers, "Somebody must have liked the *sound* of it." This conversation recalls the one between Trout and the driver of the Pyramid truck, in which that driver had the same answer for why a truck company would be named *Pyramid*. It is significant to note that although the radio advertisements in the parking lot were "lullabies" to Dwayne Hoover's ears, Trout is for some reason unable to identify advertisements that work because of the way they sound. This is a key difference between the two men: Dwayne is susceptible to advertisements, while Trout is not, instead questioning their logic.

Overpopulation

This theme is introduced clearly in Chapter 1: "They had too many people and not enough space," Vonnegut writes. "They had sold everything that was any good, and there wasn't anything to eat anymore, and still the people went on fucking." The overpopulation of the planet is linked to the theme of the destruction of the planet, since "more babies were arrivign all the time - kicking and screaming, yelling for milk."

Overpopulation is addressed again in Trout's story "This Means You," in which forty people own all the land of the Hawaiian Islands and don't allow anyone else to trespass - forcing the other inhabitants to dangle from the strings of helium balloons. Vonnegut wields allegory to demonstrate the gravity of the issue, teasing out the terrible implications of overpopulation through pop imagery and cartoon prose.

Consider also the following excerpt, from *Now It Can Be Told*:

> "The Creator of the Universe would now like to apologize not only for the capricious, jostling companionship he provided during the test, but for the trashy, stinking condition of the planet itself. The Creator programmed robots to abuse it for millions of years, so it would be a poisonous, festering cheese when you got here. Also, He made sure it would be desperately crowded by programming robots, regardless of their living conditions, to crave sexual intercourse and adore infants more than almost anything."

Race

Race is used in the characterization of every character in the book, except for the anonymous attackers who become known as *The Pluto Gang*. Thus, the speaker demonstrates his claim in Chapter 1 that "Color was everything."

Dwayne Hoover, a white "fabulously well-to-do" man, and Wayne Hoobler, a black ex-convict, are made doppelgangers by their similar names. In Chapter 14 we find out that Dwayne Hoover's stepparents originally had been named Hoobler, but had changed their last name when, in West Virginia, they realized that Hoobler was a "Nigger name." His stepfather's racism is explicit in the story Dwayne remembers in Chapter 21, which his stepfather told him when he was ten years old. It involves a black father being brutally murdered for spending the night in Shepherdstown; Dwayne's stepfather "told the story so gleefully."

Black people are likened to machines even more so than others, since white people have seen them that way since the days of slavery. For example, in Chapter 15, Dwayne is at the construction site of the new high school and asks a white worker about one of the machines. The worker tells him it is called *"The Hundred Nigger Machine"*, simultaneously referencing the common theme of humans as machines, as well as demonstrating the racism that persists in the world of the story.

But black people are also likened to animals throughout the book. Harry LeSabre and his wife Grace use the code word "reindeer" when talking about black people, and in Chapter 15 the narrator describes what they see as "the reindeer problem." Blacks were reproducing, and whites didn't see much use for them; to them there were "useless, big black animals everywhere, and a lot of them had very bad dispositions." In Chapter 18, Wayne Hoobler is likened to an animal, in that he misses prison - which recalls Bill, Trout's bird, who when freed from its cage decided to hop back inside because it was afraid of what was beyond the window.

The narrator comments on the theme of race directly in Chapter 21, when he hypothesizes:

> I think that the end of the Civil War in my country frustrated the white people in the North, who won it, in a way which has never been acknowledged before. Their descendants inherited that frustration, I think, without ever knowing what it was.
>
> The victors in that war were cheated out of the most desirable spoils of that war, which were human slaves.

When Dwayne Hoover speaks to Wayne Hoobler during his rampage, he acknowledges that "white robots were just like black robots, essentially, in that they were programmed to be whatever they were, to do whatever they did." This conclusion reconciles the idea of humans as machines with the theme of race. Thinking of humans as machines allows them all to be equal, regardless of race.

Humans as Bands of Unwavering Light

This theme is introduced by Rabo Karabekian in his defense of his painting in Chapter 19. It is contrary to the idea that so far has permeated the book, that of humans as machines. These two themes clash, but the narrator attempts to reconcile them in Chapter 20 in this description of Kilgore Trout:

> His situation, insofar as he was a machine, was complex, tragic, and laughable. But the sacred part of him, his awareness, remained an unwavering band of light.
>
> And this book is being written by a meat machine in cooperation with a machine made of metal and plastic. The plastic, incidentally, is a close relative of the gunk in Sugar Creek. And at the core of the writing meat machine is something sacred, which is an unwavering band of light.
>
> At the core of each person who reads this book is a band of unwavering light.

This passage characterizes us all, in all universes (that of Kilgore Trout, that of the narrator, or the "meat machine," and that of the readers) as having some sacred awareness that makes us unlike machines.

Birds

Birds in *Breakfast of Champions* can be read and interpreted in conjunction with the twin themes of race and the destruction of the planet. The character of Wayne Hoobler represents this connection because he, like Bill the parakeet, has been kept in cages all his life, "orphanages and youth shelters and prisons of one sort or another." He misses prison - as Bill missed his cage - since now that he is free he doesn't know what to do with himself.

This connection also builds upon the theme of race, with black people being viewed as animals thanks to the society in which they have been brought up. All the black people in Midland City can imitate birds of the British Empire, a skill they learned from Fred T. Barry's mother, who did so for her amusement. In the Epilogue, Elgin Washington asks Kilgore Trout to listen to him as he imitates a Nightingale from his hospital bed.

Machines as Living

This theme is introduced in the Epilogue as a foil to the theme of humans as machines. The reader is informed that Fred T. Barry wishes to make a museum out of the old Keedsler mansion, on the condition that the first *Robo-Magic* is exhibited, showing "how machines evolved just as animals did, but with much greater speed."

As the narrator chases Kilgore Trout, he stops running in front of the General Electric Company. The monogram and motto read, "Progress is our most important product." This motto hearkens back to the theme of advertising, now tying it to the idea that has just been introduced of machines evolving like living things. General Motors products are making "progress," just as the *Robo-Magic* evolved.

Glossary of Terms

"Breakfast of Champions"

Described in a disclaimer-type passage in the following manner:

> The expression "Breakfast of Champions" is a registered trademark of General Mills, Inc., for use on a breakfast cereal product. The use of the identical expression as the title for this book is not intended to indicate an association with or sponsorship by General Mills, nor is it intended to disparage their fine products.

This is also what Bonnie MacMahon says jokingly every time she serves a customer a martini.

"E pluribus unum"

It translates in Latin to, "Out of many, one." It is the motto of the United States, and mentioned in Chapter 1.

Bermuda Ern

Described as "the largest creatures ever to fly under their own power," these birds became extinct after men brought the athlete's foot fungus into their rookery. Trout spent his childhood measuring wingspreads of the dead birds.

BLINC

The "Blast Interval Normalization Computer," which was installed on heavy bombers to do the actual dropping of bombs during World War II. The "brain" of the *Robo-Magic* machine became the nerve center of this system.

defunct

No longer in effect or use; not operating or functioning.

In the Prologue, it is used to describe the Indianapolis times, a newspaper for which Phoebe Hurty wrote a column. In the Epilogue, it is used to describe the Monon Railroad, which used to run through the neighborhood in which the narrator accosts Trout.

Drano

A chemical used to clean drains.

free will

The faculty of being able to make one's own decisions, independent of a creator.

fuselage

The body of an airplane.

Heliogabalus

The Emperor of Rome from 218-222, whose eccentricity and debauchery led to an insurrection in which he was killed.

hypothalamus

The part of the brain that that acts as an endocrine gland by producing hormones, including the releasing factors that control the hormonal secretions of the pituitary gland. It is involved in the processes that occur within the narrator when he reacts to the attack by Kazak in the Epilogue.

incipient echolalia

The symptom of mindlessly repeating aloud whatever word or sound has just been heard. It afflicts Dwayne from the beginning of Chapter 15 on.

leak

Kilgore Trout's word for a mirror, and a motif throughout the story. Trout pretends mirrors are holes between two universes, and the narrator literally "uses" them as such.

locomotor ataxia

Also called tabes dorsalis, it is a late form of syphilis resulting in a hardening of the dorsal columns of the spinal cord and marked by shooting pains, emaciation, and loss of muscular coordination.

The narrator explains that his suspicion "that human beings are robots, are machines" stems from having seen men suffering from this disease as a boy.

Perma-Stone

A material used to plaster the sides of old houses with colored cement, to make them look as if they are made of stone.

Pluto Gang

The term given to Trout's anonymous attackers on Forty-second Street, when he innocently says, "For all I know, that car may have been occupied by an intelligent gas from Pluto."

Saint Anthony

The supposed subject of Rabo Karabekian's painting *The Temptation of Saint Anthony*, Anthony was a hermit and the Egyptian founder of Christian monasticism.

Saint Athanasius

Lived from about 296-373 AD, the Greek patriarch of Alexandria and leading defender of Christian orthodoxy against Arianism.

Saint Sebastian

A Roman soldier who was shot by archers when it was discovered that he was a secret Christian. The narrator points out that he survived the incident.

He is the subject of a painting by El Greco, featured on Mary Alice Miller's Olympic gold medal.

schizophrenia

A mental disorder characterized by some, but not necessarily all, of the following features: emotional blunting, intellectual deterioration, social isolation, disorganized speech and behavior, delusions, and hallucinations. It is also a state characterized by the coexistence of contradictory or incompatible elements, much like the universes of *Breakfast of Champions*.

The narrator does not know for certain whether he has this disorder.

Sugar Creek

The only significant surface water within eight miles of Midland City. It has become terribly polluted, and coats the feet of anyone who wades in it (including Kilgore Trout and Dwayne Hoover) in a plastic gunk.

Short Summary

Breakfast of Champions tells the story of the events that lead up to the meeting of Kilgore Trout and Dwayne Hoover, the meeting itself, and the immediate aftermath. Trout is a struggling science fiction writer who, after their fateful meeting, becomes successful and wins a Nobel Prize; Hoover is a wealthy businessman who is going insane, sent over the brink by his encounter with Trout.

Trout, who believes himself to be completely unknown as a writer, receives an invitation to the Midland City arts festival, and Trout travels to Midland City. First he goes to New York City, where he is abducted and beaten up by the only anonymous, faceless characters in the book, who through the media gain the moniker "The Pluto Gang." He hitches a ride first with a truck driver whose truck says *PYRAMID* on its side, with whom he discusses everything from politics to sex to the destruction of the planet. Then he hops a ride with the only clearly happy character in the book, the driver of a *Galaxie* who works for himself as a traveling salesman.

Dwayne Hoover gets more and more insane as the book progresses. He terrifies his employee at the Pontiac agency, Harry LeSabre, by criticizing his clothes. LeSabre is afraid Hoover has discovered that he is a closet transexual. Then he gets in a fight with his mistress and secretary, Francine Pefko because he accuses her of asking him to buy her a Kentucky Fried Chicken franchise.

Trout and Hoover meet in the cocktail lounge of the new Holiday Inn, where Hoover's homosexual and estranged son, Bunny, plays the piano. When the bartender turns on the black lights and Trout's white shirt glows brilliantly, Hoover is entranced by it. He accosts Trout and reads his novel, *Now It Can Be Told*. The premise of the novel is that there is only one creature with free will in the universe (the reader of the novel) and everyone else is a robot. Hoover interprets its message as addressed to him from the Creator of the Universe, and goes on a violent rampage, injuring many people around him and ending up in a mental hospital.

In the Epilogue, Trout is released from the hospital with a partially severed finger (Hoover has bitten it off in his rampage), and is wandering back to the arts festival, which has unbeknownst to him been canceled. The narrator, who has become an interactive character in the universe of his own creation, watches Trout and then chases him down. He proves that he is the Creator of the Universe by sending Trout all around the world, through time and back. Then he returns to his own universe, presumably, through the "void," while Trout yells after him, "Make me young!"

Throughout *Breakfast of Champions*, the reader is introduced to many minor characters as if they are major characters; the narrator points out that he means to write about life, and in life, everyone is as important a character as everyone else. He believes that the problems of the world can be traced back to humans wanting to live as if they are in a story book; this allows rulers to waste the lives of thousands of "minor" characters, and encourages people to kill one another and themselves for the effect of a dramatic ending. The narrator himself is an important character, interacting with the characters he has created and resembling Vonnegut himself in many ways.

The reader is also provided with short summaries of the works of Kilgore Trout. Their plots often demonstrate themes of *Breakfast of Champions* itself, a technique that aligns Vonnegut as an author with Trout as an author. For instance, *Plague on Wheels* deals with the extinction of a race of automobile-people. When the idea of the automobile is brought to Earth, Earthlings use it to destroy their own planet; the destruction of Earth is a theme that features frequently in *Breakfast of Champions*. Another example is "This Means You," in which a small percentage of the inhabitants of Hawaii own all the land, and decide to enforce a *No Trespassing* rule. The rest of the citizens, who do not own the land, are forced to dangle from the strings of helium balloons rather than paddle offshore. This story thus explores the theme of overpopulation (also touched upon in Trout's story *Gilgongo!*) as well as that of ownership, both of which are prominent in *Breakfast of Champions*.

Summary and Analysis of Preface and Chapters 1-4

Summary

The Preface begins with a disclaimer that the book is in no way related to the slogan "Breakfast of Champions," a registered trademark of General Mills, Inc.

Vonnegut introduces Phoebe Hurty, the Indianapolis widow to whom the book is dedicated. Vonnegut worked for her during the Great Depression, writing copy for clothes advertisements. She is important to Vonnegut because she taught him to be impolite about everything, and because she represents the hopefulness that permeated the Depression for a new American paradise that would come with prosperity.

The author explains his "suspicion" that humans are actually robots as arising from his childhood observance of men in the late stages of syphilis. This hypothesis is also supported by how much humans are affected by chemicals: Vonnegut's mother is an example of someone who "wrecked her brains" with them.

A self-analysis follows, in which Vonnegut calls the book a fiftieth-birthday present to himself and acknowledges his immaturity in illustrating the book with pictures of such things as "a Nazi flag and an asshole." His depiction of said asshole follows. He describes the book as "a sidewalk strewn with junk," since it is his attempt to "clear my head of all the junk in there."

The Preface ends with Vonnegut's announcement that he was born on Armistice Day, a day he considers sacred (along with Romeo and Juliet and "all music") because of eye-witness accounts he's heard of it. He signs the Preface -PHILBOYD STUDGE, a person about whom he earlier said, "That's who I think I am when I write what I am seemingly programmed to write."

Chapter 1 introduces the two main characters, "two lonesome, skinny, fairly old white men on a planet which was dying fast," Kilgore Trout and Dwayne Hoover. This chapter lays the foundations for their meeting. Their American nationality is important to their characters. Vonnegut situates the mindset of the American people at the time within the context of the national anthem ("which was pure balderdash"), the law against dipping the flag, "a law no other nation on the planet had about its flag," and the "vacant motto": Out of Many, One.

The speaker tells the story of the founding of America as it is taught in history classes, pointing out that "some of the nonsense was evil, since it concealed great crimes." He cites the conquistadores' murderous missions and slavery as some of those evils. Race is a huge factor in the founding of the country: "Color was everything." The "heartless," "greedy" pirates that took the land from the natives were the foundation for the country as it was when Hoover and Trout met.

The speaker then discusses the discrepancy in wealth in the world, dividing it into two groups: those who were powerful, and those who didn't have "doodley-squat." He introduces the theory of Communism as a solution to over-population, and points out that "Dwayne Hoover's and Kilgore Trout's country, where there was still plenty of everything, was opposed to Communism."

Dwayne Hoover was "fabulously well-to-do" and also addicted to chemicals that "unbalanced his mind." Combined with bad ideas, they were making him mad: "Bad chemicals and bad ideas were the Yin and Yang of madness."

Trout's science-fiction was giving Hoover the bad ideas, even though Trout was unaware of this and believed himself to have no impact on anyone else. His writing had convinced Hoover that he alone is not a robot; "everybody else was a fully automatic machine, whose purpose was to stimulate Dwayne. Dwayne was a new type of creature being tested by the Creator of the Universe."

The first chapter ends by finishing the whole story, telling how after Dwayne went to an asylum, Trout became obsessed with the notion that ideas can cause disease, as well as cure it. At first he was just "a dirty old man," but soon his ideas were taken seriously by artists and scientists alike. They even built him a monument after he died; there is a sketch of it, and engraved on it is "a quotation from his last novel, his two-hundred-and-ninth novel, which was unfinished when he died:" "We are healthy only to the extent that our ideas are humane."

Chapter 2 begins by providing a description of Dwayne's living situation: he is a widower who lives alone in a "dream house" with his dog Sparky. He also has a black servant, Lottie Davis, with whom he doesn't converse much but whom he likes.

Kilgore Trout is also alone except for a pet: his is a parakeet named Bill. This is a connection between the two men, but they talk to their pets about different things. "While Dwayne babbled to his Labrador retriever about love, Trout sneered and muttered to his parakeet about the end of the world." Trout is described as believing that humanity deserves to die horribly, since it behaves as cruelly as the Roman emperor Heliogabalus.

The speaker now introduces an important theme: that of mirrors as "leaks." Trout calls them leaks, "to pretend that mirrors were holes between two universes." This theme continues through the story, and becomes relevant at the end of the story when the speaker enters the world of his characters, transcending universes. Calling mirrors "leaks" catches on by the time of Trout's death, when he is famous and influential.

Trout is described as having no charm, while Hoover has "oodles of charm," as does the speaker. Nobody knows Trout is a writer, since he makes no copies of his work and puts little concentrated effort into getting his work published. His work is published in pornographic books and magazines, alongside "illustrations which had nothing to do with his tales." An example is the story of Delmore Skag.

Trout's most widely-distributed book was *Plague on Wheels*. It was published under the banner "Wide-Open Beavers Inside!" The speaker explains that a "wide-open beaver was a photograph of a woman not wearing underpants, and with her legs far apart, so that the mouth of her vagina could be seen." The speaker explains the origin of the euphemism "beaver," and draws sketches of the two kinds of beavers (an animal and a vagina). Wide-open beavers are described as "the most massively defended secret under law," comparably unattainable to girls' underpants for little boys.

Kilgore Trout's Nobel Prize speech in 1979 references the rhyme, "I See England/I see France/I see a little girl's/Underpants!" Vonnegut uses this anecdote to hint at the state of the world in 1979: England and France are "two nations which no longer existed as such," and "human beings are now the only animals left on earth." This hinting at the future by embedding details in anecdotes is common throughout the book.

Now the story of *Plague on Wheels* is revealed: it's about life on a dying planet named *Lingo-Three*, where the people are actually automobiles with wheels. Visiting space travelers (homosexual, inch-high people from the planet Zeltoldimar) discover that the automobile-people have destroyed the resources on *Lingo-Three*. The space travelers cannot save the automobile-people, since their eggs are too heavy to bring back to Zeltoldimar; their spokesman, Kago, says, "You will be gone, but not forgotten." The space travelers leave *Lingo-Three* and later arrive on Earth. They tell the Earthlings about the automobiles that are dying out on *Lingo-Three*, and unknowingly bring about the destruction of the Earthlings because, "human beings could be as easily felled by a single idea as by cholera or the bubonic plague." This is another important theme: ideas as disease.

The speaker again uses the technique of hinting at the future of Earth, by using Trout's story: "Ideas on Earth were badges of friendship or enmity. Their content did not matter... And then Earthlings discovered tools. Suddenly agreeing with friends could be a form of suicide or worse." But Earthlings continue agreeing with each other, "being friendly when they should have been thinking instead," governed by ideas. This is the reason that ideas can spread like disease.

Chapter 3 continues the description of *Plague on Wheels*, Trout's story that was introduced at the end of Chapter 2. It reveals the fate of Earth after the introduction of the automobile: "Every form of life on that once peaceful and moist and nourishing blue-green ball was dying or dead. Everywhere were the shells of the great beetles which men had made and worshiped. They were automobiles. They had killed everything."

Next we are introduced to Eliot Rosewater, the writer of Trout's only fan mail before 1972. Trout concludes from the writing that Rosewater must be a teenager, a misconception which he retains throughout the story. The letter says that Trout should be made president of the United States; but that would be impossible, since Trout was born in Bermuda. His father, Leo Trout, guarded the only nesting place in the world for Bermuda Erns. The Ern is a symbol that is continued throughout the story, along with that of birds in general. Trout "had seen those Erns die, one by one." They were the largest creatures to fly on the planet, but were now extinct because of athlete's foot, which was brought to their rookery by men and which eventually killed the Erns. Kilgore's task as a boy was to measure the wingspans of the Ern corpses, a job which is identified as leading to his life-long melancholy.

Kilgore then receives a letter from Fred T. Barry, the chairman of a festival celebrating the opening of the Mildred Barry Memorial Center for the Arts in Midland City. Fred T. Barry says that Trout was recommended to the festival by Eliot Rosewater, and includes a check for $1000 with the invitation. Trout is suspicious at these two letters, since he doesn't want strangers "tampering with the privacy of his body bag." Trout pulls out his old tuxedo, which he hasn't worn since senior prom, and which is covered in mold.

Then Trout decides to make Bill's biggest three wishes come true. He opens the door to the parakeet's cage, and Bill flies over to the windowsill. "There was just one layer of glass between Bill and the great out-of-doors." Then Trout opens the window, but Bill flies back inside his cage. Trout says to Bill, "That's the most intelligent use of three wishes I ever heard of. You made sure you'd still have something worth wishing for - to get out of the cage."

Trout argues with himself about whether or not to attend the festival, and finally decides to go, telling Bill: "Listen, I'm leaving the cage, but I'm coming back." He hitchhikes to New York City in order to buy some of his books in pornography stores there, so he can read out of them at the festival in Midland City. He wants to tell them what he hopes to have on his tombstone: "Somebody [Sometime to Sometime] He Tried."

Chapter 4 returns to Dwayne, who "was meanwhile getting crazier all the time." So far, he has been behaving acceptably in public. Vonnegut uses the technique of foreshadowing by revealing what people would say later, after Dwayne "ran amok." Dwayne has begun to sing to himself, which makes his secretary, Francine Pefko, think he is getting happier and happier rather than crazier and crazier. Harry LeSabre, Dwayne's sales manager, notices that Dwayne is going crazy a week before he "went off his rocker," and mentions it to Francine.

The speaker explains how Dwayne bought a Pontiac agency so cheaply: he borrowed it from the bank, putting up stock in a company called *The Midland City Ordnance Company*. When he bought the stock, it was called *The Robo-Magic Corporation of America*. Harry LeSabre and Vernon Garr are identified as the only two employees who have been with Dwayne since the agency was in a "Nigger part of town."

Dwayne was never in combat, but as a civilian employee of the US Army Air Corps during WWII, he got to paint a message on the side of a bomb. There is a drawing of the bomb with the message on its side, which reads: "Goodbye Blue Monday." The meaning of this symbol won't be explained till the end of the story, but the repetition of the phrase "Goodbye Blue Monday" in this chapter makes clear that the reader should be on the look out for significance in it.

Harry goes into Dwayne's office and makes small talk, and happens to mention adoption. Dwayne snaps, since he himself was adopted. He berates Harry for his boring wardrobe. This is why Harry mentions to Francine that Dwayne seems strange, since this kind of starkly mean behavior is unusual. Francine reminds him that Dwayne is "the best employer in town," and doesn't think it's a big deal.

Hawaiian Week is approaching; it's a sales promotion scheme that enters customers into a lottery to go to Hawaii, and involves decorating the agency like the islands. Dwayne mentions it as impetus for Harry to change the way he dresses. Harry is especially offended by Dwayne's behavior because he is a secret transvestite; only his wife knows about it. Harry now worries that Dwayne is threatening him.

That weekend is Veterans' Day weekend; Veterans' Day has already been signaled out by Vonnegut as "not sacred" in the Preface. Dwayne's "bad chemicals" make him stick a gun in his mouth. But instead of shooting himself, he instead shoots up one of his bathrooms. He shoots a picture of a flamingo (drawing provided), and "snarled at the recollection of it afterwards. Here is what he snarled: 'Dumb fucking bird.'"

Dwayne goes outside to play basketball, and his dog, Sparky, watches him. Then he jumps into his car and goes on a dangerous ride, going backwards and jumping a curb, finally stopping in a vacant lot that he happens to own. Nobody observes any of this behavior. This is an important link between Trout and Hoover: Trout feels like nobody knows he exists, and Hoover has just acted insanely and nobody knows.

Analysis

The Preface introduces the important theme of humans as machines, and Chapter 2 expands upon this theme, specifically representing humans as cars in *Plague on Wheels*. This story by Trout not only reflects the narrator's opinion of humans as machines, it also hints at another major theme of *Breakfast of Champions*, which is the destruction of the planet. The preface presents the theme of humans as machines alongside the idea of humans wrecking their brains with chemicals; this connection proves to be important to the story, since Dwayne, one of the characters who is pointed out as using "chemicals" regularly, meets his downfall when he becomes convinced that all other inhabitants of Earth are robots.

Chapter 1 likewise lays out a few themes that will be important throughout the story. First, the theme of the emotional state of Americans is introduced when the narrator states that many Americans are "so ignored and cheated and insulted that they thought they might be in the wrong country, or even on the wrong planet, that some terrible mistake had been made." This description is later applied to the character of Wayne Hoobler in particular; it is also used to personify animals, for example the dog, Lancer, whose excrement ends up on Kilgore Trout's jacket.

Chapter 1 also introduces the theme of ownership, by generally dividing Americans into the groups of "fabulously well to do" and those who don't have "doodley squat." This theme will play itself out through Trout's story, "This Means You," as well as through the descriptions of several characters - for example, the homeless people on *Skid Row*, where Bunny Hoover lives, as compared to Eliot Rosewater and his family, who own the oil under all the land in West Virginia.

Chapters 3 and 4 provide a groundwork for the theme of birds, which is tied to that of the destruction of the planet, and which appears throughout the story. The Bermuda Ern, which becomes extinct because of the spreading of the human strand of disease, athlete's foot, is a recurring reference. The interaction between Trout and his parakeet makes stark the comparison between Bill, the caged bird who ultimately chooses to remain caged, and the Erns, the huge extinct species from Bermuda. Trout personifies Bill by linking his own situation in fearing the arts festival to that of the bird: "I'm not going, Bill. I don't want out of my cage." Bill will later be compared to Wayne Hoobler, who has been caged his whole life in various prisons, and doesn't know what to do with himself now that he's released. A third bird symbol is the inanimate flamingo in the bathroom that Dwayne shoots. The Erns flew free but were made extinct by disease; Bill is given the opportunity to be free but opts to stay in his cage; and the flamingo in the bathroom is never alive, but is shot all the same by Dwayne.

The motto of *The Robo-Magic Corporation of America*, which is "Goodbye, Blue Monday," as well as *The Robo-Magic* itself, are prominent motifs that are introduced here. "Goodbye, Blue Monday" takes on various implied meanings throughout the story, finally being shouted by an incoherent Dwayne in the ambulance, as the ultimate random phrase to baffle his Creator. The *Robo-Magic* becomes a symbol of both advertising and race, linking the two in its original advertising scheme, in which it is lauded as doing the "Nigger work" of washing clothes.

Summary and Analysis of Chapters 5-8

Summary

Kilgore Trout is trying to sleep in a movie theater in New York City, precisely because he knows "sleeping in movie houses was the sort of thing really dirty old men did." He wants to embody that persona when he arrives in Midland City. He has spent the day visiting pornography shops, where he bought two of his own books, *Plague on Wheels* and *Now It Can Be Told*. The latter is the book that ends up turning Dwayne Hoover "into a homicidal maniac."

He also buys a pornographic magazine including one of his stories, "The Dancing Fool." The premise of the story is that a flying saucer creature named Zog arrives on Earth from the planet Margo, where everyone communicates by means of farting and tap dancing. He tries to explain to Earthlings how to prevent wars and cure cancer, but they don't understand his farting and tap dancing so they kill him.

While Trout watches the pornographic movie that is playing the theater (because it is that kind of theater), he makes up another novel. It is about an astronaut from Earth named Don who goes to a planet where pollution has killed everything except humanoids. The humaniods are bothered because their movie theaters only show dirty movies - but when they take Don to see the dirty movies, the theme is about eating. The movies consist of close-ups of people eating different types of food; sex is equated to food in this way. After the movie, Don the astronaut goes out into the street and is accosted by whores offering "eggs and oranges and milk and butter and peanuts and so on. The whores couldn't actually deliver these goodies, of course."

Chapter 6 takes us back to Dwayne Hoover, sitting in his car in the parking lot he owns in Midland City. We are told that while Dwayne sat there so alone, Mary Young, the oldest inhabitant of Midland City was dying in the County Hospital, also alone. The only person with her while she dies is a black intern, Cyprian Ukwende.

Dwayne now drives to the new Holiday Inn next door to his Pontiac agency and goes up to the roof. He gazes out over the city and says, "Where am I?" This is significant because Midland City is where Dwayne has always been - he was born and adopted there, went to school there, and now he owns almost everything in the town. He seems to forget everything, even that his wife, Celia Hoover, committed suicide and that his son, Bunny, is a homosexual. The chapter ends with him repeating, "Where am I?"

Chapter 7 begins in the men's room of the movie house, where Trout sees this message written on the tiled wall: "What is the purpose of life?" He cannot write a response because he has no writing utensil, but wants to write: "To be the eyes and ears and conscience of the Creator of the Universe, you fool." When he returns to the theater, the only person there is the ticket-taker/bouncer/janitor, sweeping. He tells

Trout to go home. Before leaving, Trout examines the box in the back of the auditorium that can be flicked on to start the movie. There is a drawing of an on/off switch. "It intrigued Trout to know that he had only to flick the switch, and the people would start fucking and sucking again."

Chapter 8 begins with Trout exiting onto Forty-second Street, which is dangerous, just like the whole city "because of chemicals and the uneven distribution of wealth and so on." The theater manager follows Trout out of the theater and locks the door, and then "two young black prostitutes materialized from nowhere." They had grown up in the rural south, "where their ancestors had been used as agricultural machinery."

We are given a summary of Trout's story called "This Means You," about forty people who own all the land of the Hawaiian Islands, and who "exercise their property rights to the full." Since no one else is allowed to trespass on the property, there is nowhere for them to stand. The Federal Government solves the problem by providing a helium balloon to each person, so they can hover above the land without trespassing.

Trout and the manager refuse the services of the prostitutes, and walk together until Trout is attacked. His attackers are mysterious, since the only thing he notices is their white Olds-mobile *Toronado* with a black vinyl roof. When he comes to, he has been beaten up, robbed, and his pants and underpants are around his ankles. The police find him while he is pulling up his pants and they bring him to the hospital, where it is discovered that he is not seriously injured. When asked what his attackers look like, Trout responds, "For all I know, they may not even have been Earthlings. For all I know, that car may have been occupied by an intelligent gas from Pluto." His saying this is significant, because his attackers are perhaps the first characters in the book unidentified by the color of their skin. The speaker has always specifed "black" or "white" in characterizations, but these attackers are anonymous. It implies that all inhabitants of the city are equally likely to attack and beat an old man for his money.

Trout's words are blown out of proportion: "his comment turned out to be the first germ in an epidemic of mind-poisoning." The "disease" is spread by a reporter who writes a story about the attack under the headline: "PLUTO BANDITS KIDNAP PAIR." *The Pluto Gang* becomes known among New Yorkers, who fear it because it is something specific to fear. A group of Puerto Rican boys who wish "to become frightening, in order to defend themselves and their friends and families" decide to adopt the moniker.

Analysis

The novel that Trout begins to write in Chapter 5 hints at the theme of the destruction of the planet, but points out that Earth isn't the only planet with problems. The humanoids on the planet where sex is equated to food have destroyed everything with pollution, just as humans are doing on Earth.

The sense of isolation Dwayne feels at the end of Chapter 6 can be compared to that which Trout feels at the beginning of the story. Trout then feels that nobody knows who he is, and now Dwayne feels he has forgotten who he is. He loses his identity, an ironic development as he is a symbol of ownership (being "fabulously well to do"). Even looking down upon a city in which he owns nearly every building, he cannot find within it or the view a sense of self. This dilemma also draws attention to the multiple universes that exist within the story; Dwayne's self-directed question could be expanded in scope to the following query: "What universe am I in?"

In the pornographic movie house, Trout's thought about turning on the movies again recalls the theme of humans as machines. The people in the pornographic movie can be made to perform the most basic of human functions simply by the flip of a switch. Human flesh is reduced to buttons and pulleys, tricks of light, chemicals; human agency is reduced to automation.

Summary and Analysis of Chapters 9-12

Summary

Dwayne Hoover comes down from the roof of the new Holiday Inn to ask for a room. He gets in line behind Cyprian Ukwende, who was staying at the Inn until he found an apartment. Dwayne waits in line, even though he owns the hotel, and then enters his room. He adores it because it is "so new and cool and clean." He feels accomplished for having "delivered himself to an irreproachable container for a human being." He finds comfort in this anonymity, and explores the different amenities of the room. Then he sleeps like a lamb.

Chapter 10 returns to Kilgore Trout, who is released by the police and gets a ride from a truck. The driver is white, and says he used to be a hunter and fisherman. Trout responds by saying that he, too, used to be a conservationist, before he realized that "God wasn't any conservationist, so for anybody else to be one was sacrilegious and a waste of time." The driver is impressed. They talk about Vietnam and suicide, but then the driver becomes annoyed with Trout because he can't tell if he's being serious or not. To pass the time, Trout makes up a story called "Gilgongo!" about a planet in which there is too much creation going on. The driver brings up politics, and Trout has no interest in politicians. He had once written a story about a chimpanzee who became President of the United States.

The driver and Trout stop the eat, and when the driver says "Excuse me, I've got to take a leak," Trout uses his joke that where he comes from in Bermuda, mirrors are called leaks. The driver will tell his wife about it.

Trout then notices that the truck he has been riding in says PYRAMID in huge letters on the side. He sees it through the eyes of a child, and decides it must be very important because it was written so big. He does the same for another truck, whose side reads AJAX. These observations will be tied to the theme of mindless advertising later.

In Chapter 11, Dwayne Hoover has slept until 10am in the new Holiday Inn, and feels refreshed. He eats breakfast in the restaurant of the Inn, at the table over from Cyprian Ukwende. He looks out at the flat land - "flat city, flat township, flat county, flat state," and thinks about Sugar Creek.

Then he ventures outside, suspecting that he might be cured from his mental disease. But as soon as he steps outside, he feels like the asphalt of he Pontiac agency has turned into a kind of trampoline, sinking beneath his weight. He sees a young black man named Wayne Hoobler, a parolee from prison. Wayne Hoobler is "burnishing" one of the cars on Dwayne Hoover's used car lot, trying to make a good impression because he wants to work for Dwayne. But Dwayne just shakes his head vaguely and walks inside to the showroom.

The showroom is decorated for Hawaiian week, but Dwayne is confused because he forgets about the themed week. He sees Harry LeSabre wearing a ridiculous Hawaiian costume, since the previous week Dwayne had berated him for his plain clothing. Harry and his wife have been debating whether or not Dwayne suspects that he is a transvestite, and they have come to the conclusion that Dwayne cannot know. Harry approaches Dwayne now, "rosy with fear and excitement," and says "Aloha."

Chapter 12 returns to Trout, who is still in the Pyramid truck, crossing into Philadelphia. The driver and Trout talk about how neither of them is a veteran, and then the driver confides that he has no friends because he's always on the road. He wants it to be true that Trout has "a rich social life so that he could enjoy it vicariously," but Trout just shrugs. He has forgotten the driver's name.

Now Vonnegut uses the first-person speaker again, in the technique of direct address. He tells us, "Trout had a mental defect which I, too, used to suffer from. He couldn't remember what different people in his life looked like - unless their bodies or faces were strikingly unusual." For example, the only person he calls by name in his hometown of Cohoes is Durling Heath, a "red-headed Cockney midget" who works in a shoe repair shop.

The driver continues to talk about how lonesome life on the road is, and concludes that, "That's probably the story of my life: not enough determination." They talk about *Perma-Stone*, a colored cement that is plastered on houses to make them look as if they are made of stone. Trout's company sells it, and they talk about it as if they are on a commercial. This exchange demonstrates how much commercial advertising has permeated life.

Trout now asks the driver why the company is called *Pyramid*. He thinks it doesn't make sense, since the truck moves quickly and pyramids don't move at all. Trout is very confused by this naming. The driver responds, "He liked the *sound* of it. Don't you like the *sound* of it?" Trout agrees just "to keep things friendly," then creates a little story in his head. It is about a planet where the creatures were so "enchanted by sounds" that the language kept turning into music.

The driver asks about Trout's family, and Trout's characterization is furthered for the reader through this conversation. We discover that Trout has been married three times, and that he has one son, Leo, who left home at the age of fourteen and has not contacted Kilgore since. Then Kilgore had heard that Leo had deserted in Viet Nam and joined the Viet Cong.

Analysis

Many salient themes are touched upon in these chapters. In Chapter 10, the driver of the Pyramid truck makes the point that "the planet was being destroyed by manufacturing processes, and what was being manufactured was lousy, by and large." This point of view implies a dismal future for the planet as a result of all the damage humans are inflicting on it.

Trout's stories emerge here as allegories, refracting Vonnegut's favorite themes through the prism of Trout's own eccentric imagination. This in a sense allows Vonnegut more free rein, at least in formal terms. The story that Trout makes up to pass the time, "Gilgongo!," is about a planet in which there is too much creation going on. It addresses the theme of overpopulation, which has been explored in Trout's other story, "This Means You," in Chapter 8. The story Trout remembers writing about the chimpanzee leads us down a different road: Vonnegut seems to be positing that sometimes the president is so useless, and fails so miserably at solving the problems that plague Americans, it would be just the same if he were a chimpanzee. Again, Trout's stories use hyperbole to express a point.

The theme of mirrors as "leaks" between universes resurfaces when Trout tells the driver that where he comes from in Bermuda, mirrors are called "leaks." This passing of false information once again demonstrates the ability of ideas to spread like disease. Though of course, thinking a mirror is called a leak in Bermuda is not a damaging idea, and not disease itself, this spreading of false information demonstrates the theme.

When Trout asks the driver why the truck company is called *Pyramid*, the driver responds that the person who named it "liked the *sound* of it. Don't you like the *sound* of it?" This question, as well as the following story Trout makes up about a planet where the creatures were so "enchanted by sounds" that the language kept turning into music, hints at the theme of advertising. In the story, the creatures' enchantment with sounds was a problem since the music was useless as a conveyor of information, so the leaders had to keep inventing "new and much uglier vocabularies and sentence structures all the time, which would resist being transmuted to music." This story hearkens back to the advertisements that were "like lullabyes" to Dwayne Hoover's ears in Chapter 4. It is a significant character trait that the advertisements are music to Dwayne's ears, while Trout cannot understand "liking the sound" of something as justification for a ridiculous name of a company.

The relationship between Trout and his son, Leo, is comparable to that between Dwayne and his son, Bunny, in that both are estranged. Trout tells the truck driver that his son joined the Viet Cong; this seemingly ridiculous event ties into the theme of Communism. The Viet Cong is a Communist group, so it is fitting that Trout's offspring should join it: Trout himself has "doodley-squat," and his son joins a movement that believes all things should be shared. Interestingly, Leo Trout is the narrator of another of Vonnegut's books, *Galapagos*.

Summary and Analysis of Chapters 13-14

Summary

Harry LeSabre has been "destroyed by Dwayne." Dwayne had reacted to Harry's Hawaiian costume as if he could not see it, because he had forgotten it was Hawaiian week and just thought it was his insanity acting up. But Harry took this reaction to mean that Dwayne knew he was a transvestite, and that he was fired because of it. Dwayne is oblivious to the effect he has had on Harry.

Francine tells Dwayne that his twin, younger step-brothers, Lyle and Kyle Hoover, are waiting for him in the inner office. They own the Sacred Miracle Cave, a tourist trap, along with Dwayne. The underground stream that runs through the Sacred Miracle Cave was polluted by industrial waste "which formed bubbles as big as ping-pong balls," that were taking over the attraction by engulfing it. The twins tell Dwayne that they had done an experiment in which they shot the bubbles, and they let loose a "stink you wouldn't believe-" they smelled like athlete's foot.

The Sacred Miracle cave is described as having been discovered in 1937 by Dwayne Hoover. The farm on which they discovered it was started by Josephus Hoobler, and ex-slave, and came to be owned by Dwayne's stepfather. It was called Bluebird Farm, but Dwayne's stepfather called it "...a God damn Nigger farm," and "ripped a Nigger sign off the Nigger mailbox, and he threw it into a ditch." The sign read, "Bluebird Farm."

In Chapter 14, Kilgore Trout has reached West Virginia, whose surface "had been demolished by men and machinery and explosives in order to make it yield up its coal. The coal was mostly gone now." Trout wonders aloud what people do for fun in West Virginia, and the driver of the Pyramid truck answers that he doesn't know, but one night he observed people at a roller rink.

Next, we as readers are taken on a tour of the images that pop up in Trout's head, through Vonnegut's use of stream of consciousness. But rather than a stream of Trout's consciousness, it is a stream of the speaker's consciousness, blending the division between the universe of the speaker and that of his characters. Trout thinks about how quickly all the coal energy of West Virginia had been used up by white men, and how it had powered old-fashioned steamboats and choo-choo trains. There is a picture of what their whistles looked like. They made a sound like "mating or dying dinosaurs." There is a picture of a dinosaur, and of a pea, which is equal to the size of both of a dinosaur's brains combined. Trout thinks that maybe the whistles' cries went into outer space along with the heat energy they produced, but he is incorrect, the speaker note, since "the atmosphere of Earth relative to the planet wasn't even as thick as the skin of an apple." There is a picture of an apple. The speaker then notes that the driver was a "big eater," especially of hamburgers. There is a picture of a cow, since that is the animal of which hamburgers are made. Then there is a picture of the "finished product," a hamburger.

At this point, the reader is to assume that the driver and Trout have arrived at a burger joint. Trout orders a cup of coffee and starts a conversation with a very old miner on a stool next to him. The old miner used to work for Rosewater Coal and Iron Company, owned by Eliot Rosewater's family.

When they're back on the road, the driver asks why on earth Trout is going to Midland City, calling it "the asshole of the Universe." Trout lies and says his sister is sick. The driver has serendipitously read *The Barring-gaffner of Bagnialto* or *This Year's Masterpiece*, by Kilgore Trout. This happened because he had been jailed for speeding in nearby Libertyville. The main industry there was making new paper out of old magazines and newspapers and books, and since the unloading process was sloppy, bits and pieces of literature were flying all over town. They used books for toilet paper in jail, and the driver happened to read the toilet paper that was *The Barring-gaffner of Bagnialto,* or *This Year's Masterpiece*.

The driver points out that all the mailboxes in the area have the name "Hoobler" on them. This is, incidentally, the last name of Wayne Hoobler, the ex-convict. It is revealed that Dwayne Hoover's stepparents had originally been named Hoobler, but when they moved to Midland City, they had their name legally changed so it wouldn't be the same as all the black people name Hoobler.

Analysis

The pollution bubbles destroying Sacred Miracle Cave demonstrate the theme of the destruction of the planet by drawing attention to humans' destruction of *themselves*. Sacred Miracle Cave is a man-made tourist trap, and it too is subject to destruction. The fact that the pollution bubbles smell like athlete's foot is significant because it draws a connection to another symbol associated with the theme of pollution: the extinct Ern in Bermuda. The Ern became extinct because it was attacked by the athlete's foot virus.

The name of the farm that Dwayne's stepfather bought, "Bluebird Farm," is important, since it includes both the color blue (most notably of the phrase, "Goodbye, Blue Monday") as well as the word bird, which we have seen as a symbol of entrapment versus freedom. The ex-slave who founded the farm named it after this symbol, the bird, but lost his farm in the Great Depression and it eventually came to be owned by someone who hated his race. Even though Josephus Hoobler had been freed as a slave, his race continued to hinder his success.

The description of West Virginia in the beginning of Chapter 14 further references the theme of the destruction of the planet. West Virginia is a symbol of the total dessication of the land - it is "collapsing into all the holes which had been dug into it." It represents the future of the whole Earth, in accordance with the them of its destruction. The description the truck driver gives of the West Virginians he observed in the roller rink likens humans to machinery: "They went around and around. Nobody smiled. They just went around and around." Vonnegut even puts these dismal humans on wheels, to reinforce their connection to the machinery that has destroyed their state.

The interaction that Trout has with the old miner in Chapter 14 links the theme of the destruction of the planet to the theme of ownership and disenfranchisement of Americans. When Trout asks what it's like to work for such a destructive industry, the old miner answers that he's too tired to care. He becomes a symbol of the working class in America, too tired to care about their work or its impact. The emotional state of Americans is linked to the theme of ownership, since the reason the old miner doesn't care is that it "don't matter if you care, if you don't own what you care about." The old miner used to work for Rosewater Coal and Iron Company, owned by Eliot Rosewater's family.

The Barring-gaffner of Bagnialto, or *This Year's Masterpiece*, the book of Trout's that the driver happens to have read, is an allegory of the work of Rabo Karabekian. The book takes place on the planet *Bagnialto*, and it is told from the point of view of a cobbler named Gooz. On the planet *Bagnialto*, citizens submit works of art to a government official called a "Barring-gaffner," who spins a wheel to randomly decide cash values for the art. Gooz submits the only picture he's ever painted, of his cat, and it randomly gets assigned the worth of one billion dollars. The story ends with the discovery that the wheel was rigged, and the barring-gaffer's subsequent suicide. This story is an allegory that can be aligned with the painting of Rabo Karabekin, who will be introduced later. This story reflects Karabekian's painting, which was sold to Midland City for $50,000. This is resented by most citizens, who consider it to be a worthless piece of art. *The Barring-gaffner of Bagnialto,* or *This Year's Masterpiece* comments upon the arbitrary values assigned to "masterpieces" like Karabekian's.

Summary and Analysis of Chapters 15-17

Summary

Dwayne Hoover drives to lunch, and is now experiencing a new symptom: incipient echolalia, or wanting to "repeat out loud whatever had just been said." Wayne Hoobler is still loitering around the Pontiac dealership, hiding from employees. While Dwayne eats lunch, the narrator discusses how "bad chemicals" were common throughout history, as demonstrated by those who assassinated John F. Kennedy, as well as by the Nazis.

Dwayne's waitress, Patty Keene, is described as a "brand-new adult," who is burdened by the hospital bills her father racked up before dying. Vonnegut uses this character to express another characteristic of America cynically, which is that everyone must pay their own bills, even when those bills are just for the misfortune of getting sick. Patty decides to have a conversation with Dwayne, because she is aware of how rich he is and thinks maybe he can solve her financial problems. When Dwayne repeats her final word, "buzzed," she becomes self-conscious and apologizes for her use of language. Patty was raped by Don Breedlove in the parking lot of the Bannister Memorial Fieldhouse, named for George Hickman Bannister. He was a teenager who had been killed while playing football in 1924 on Thanksgiving Day. In fact, there were two monuments erected in his honor, although "nobody ever thought about him anymore." Dwayne and Patty have a short conversation, and when he leaves Burger Chef, she believes she can win him over.

The narrator discusses how he has recently heard about the proof of the tectonic plate theory, but how neither Patty nor Dwayne knows about it yet. The narrator uses direct address, making himself even more of a character in his own story: "I only found out about it day before yesterday. I was reading a magazine, and I also had the television on."

The narrator now begins talking about the size of the male characters' penises. From this point on, he often uses penis size in characterizations. We immediately learn about the penis sizes of Dwayne Hoover, his son Bunny, Kilgore Trout, Harry LeSabre, Cyprian Ukwende, and Don Breedlove. The narrator then moves on to Patty Keene's hip, waist, and bosom measurements, and also provides those for Dwayne's late wife, Francine Pefko, and Dwayne's step-mother.

Dwayne wanders over to the construction site of the new high school. He asks a white workman about a machine, and the workman replies that they call it "*The Hundred-Nigger Machine*," which the narrator explains references "a time when black men had done most of the heavy digging in Midland City."

Dwayne returns to work and avoids everyone because he is embarrassed by his tendency to repeat the last word he hears. He calls Francine on the phone and asks her to come with him to the Quality Motor Court at Shepherdstown. She asks Gloria Browning, the white cashier in the Service Department, to cover her desk. Dwayne has been reading about how to be a better lover, in order to repay Francine for her loyalty. Vonnegut uses this fact as a lead-in to a description of one of Trout's stories, called *The Son of Jimmy Valentine*.

Jimmy Valentine had extrasensitive fingertips, and he worked as a safe-cracker. His son, Ralston Valentine, also had extrasensitive fingertips, but instead was amazing at touching women sexually. He was elected President of the United States, thanks to his skills in bed. The description of this story draws attention to the theme of women's sexuality being forbidden, which we were introduced to in Chapter 1. Vonnegut reveals it as ridiculous through the character of Ralston Valentine, showing that women make up enough of the population to elect a president, and that their sexuality is clearly important to them, so it ought not to be ignored.

Dwayne and Francine make love, and Francine tells him that she loves him, even though she has promised not to. The description of Francine's history that follows allows us to understand her better as a character: she is extremely loyal to men, and after her husband, Robert, died in Viet Nam, she became dedicated to Dwayne. Dwayne and Francine discuss the use of the electric chair, and Dwayne remembers recent famous electrocutions. Then Francine makes the mistake of thinking aloud, absentmindedly, that "this would be a very good location for a Colonel Sanders Kentucky Fried Chicken franchise." Dwayne assumes that Francine is hinting that she wants him to buy her one, and he wants her to "love him for his body and soul, not for what his money could buy." He had been relaxed, but becomes tense again, and berates her for asking for a gift. Francine is extremely upset, because she loves him so much and is desperately loyal to him. He is unjustly nasty to her, and she realizes that Harry LeSabre was right when he mentioned how nasty Dwayne had suddenly become.

Harry LeSabre is, incidentally, crying at this moment, too, because he feels his has lost Dwayne Hoovers good opinion. His wife, Grace, is smoking a cigar and reassuring him by scorning Dwayne and his marriage with his late wife. Harry and his wife use the code word "reindeer" to refer to black people, and at this moment, specifically to their black maid. Grace suggests moving to Maui, and they do.

Dwayne is being comforted by Francine, and he tells her about a trip he made to the headquarters of the Pontiac Division of General Motors, three months after his wife's death. He had witnessed the destruction of Pontiacs by scientists, and comments that "Everything you're not supposed to do to a car, they did to a car." The sign on the door read, *Destructive Testing*. In order to comfort him, Francine suggests he attend the arts festival as a type of therapy, since he refuses to see a doctor. "This was a bad mistake," the narrator informs us, in a use of dramatic irony. The characters don't know what they are in for, but we the readers know how catastrophic Dwayne's interaction with the arts will be.

Kilgore Trout is still hitchhiking westward, and is now a pasenger in a Ford *Galaxie*, driven by a traveling salesman named Andy Lieber. The chapter ends with a brief description of one of Trout's novels, called *How You Doin'?*, about national averages and their use in advertising campaigns on another planet.

Chapter 16 begins by continuing the story of Trout's novel *How You Doin'?*, in which the eaters of peanut butter from Earth are attempting to conquer the "shazzbutter" eaters from another planet. In order to do so, they use the averages system of the advertising campaign to make all the listeners feel *below* average, and thus lower their self-esteem. It is much easier to conquer them this way.

Trout is still in the *Galaxie*, and notices that it has a fire extinguisher with the brand name *Excelsior*. He asks the driver of the *Galaxie* why he thinks it is named that, and the driver shrugs and answers, "Somebody must have liked the *sound* of it." Trout notices a sign advertising Sacred Miracle Cave, which is owned by Kyle and Lyle Hoover. The sign is used as a transition into the connection between Trout and Dwayne Hoover: Trout thumbs through his book *Now It Can Be Told*, the one that will "turn Dwayne into a homicidal maniac." The book is in the form of a letter from the Creator of the Universe to the reader, named The Man, who is an experimental creature. All other creatures lack The Man's free will faculty, and are merely robots. The Man is transferred to a virgin planet, where he is Adam and the sea is Eve. Cells from his palms are mixed with the sea to create evolving, complicated life forms, all with free will. The man bathes in the sea and then jumps into an icy mountain stream; as he emerges, he thinks of something to yell. "The Creator never knew what he was going to yell, since the Creator had no control over him." The Man's tombstone reads: "Not Even The Creator of the Universe Knew What The Man Was Going to Say Next. Perhaps The Man Was a Better Universe in its Infancy."

Chapter 17 is about Bunny Hoover, Dwayne's son. He is dressing for work; he is the piano player in the lounge of the new Holiday Inn. A vegetarian, he also has no friends. While he plays the piano, he practices Transcendental Meditation, which allows him to "become a skin diver in the depths of his mind." While he meditates, he sees a single word "floating by lazily, a translucent, scarf-like fish." The word is "Blue;" this is significant because he learned that pornographic movies are also called "blue" movies; both the movies and Bunny's homosexual lifestyle are offensive to the mind of the America in this story. It is also a reference to the phrase "Goodbye, Blue Monday," which was the motto of the company which Dwayne Hoover mortgaged in order to buy the Pontiac Dealership. Another "lovely scarf" floats by in Bunny's consciousness, this one reading, "Clair de Lune." Vonnegut provides sketches of both scarves.

Now we are provided with a biography of Bunny, in which Vonnegut uses the technique of direct address to liken the narrator to this character. Bunny was sent away to military school when he told his father, Dwayne, that he wished he were a woman. His mother, like the narrator's mother, committed suicide. The narrator also points out that both women were petrified of having their pictures taken. The importance of this connection is made prominent by what happens afterward: "Bunny smiled at himself in the mirror, in the *leak*." By having Bunny do this, it is as if the narrator acknowledges the connection between the two universes, and foreshadows the breach that is about to happen, when he will become part of the characters' universe.

Bunny's window looks out to the old Opera House, which became *The Bannister*, a motion picture house, which then became the gangster-controlled Empire Furniture Company. Bunny lives on Skid Row, and the narrator points out that every city has a neighborhood like it. It is where homeless people, who are described as "as easy to move, usually, as toy balloons," are sent; they "drift hither and yon, like balloons filled with some gas slightly heavier than air, until they came to rest in Skid Row..." this description is important because it links the homeless people in Skid Rows all over America to the characters in Trout's story, *This Means You*. Those characters were forced to dangle from the strings of balloons, because the owners of all the land of the Hawaiian Islands enforced a *No Trespassing* rule. The enforcement of this theme of ownership (or lack thereof) demonstrates the narrator's disgust with the treatment of those who own nothing in America. Vonnegut almost instructs us as readers to make this connection, since he follows the description of Skid Row with one of Trout's other stories, in which a town tells derelicts where to go by directing them to Skid Row with signs.

Bunny makes the connection between his universe and that of the narrator clear by smiling at himself in the mirror/leak. Then he calls himself to attention, becoming "the insufferably brainless, humorless, heartless soldier he had learned to be in military school." He repeats the motto he had learned, there: "Can do." It is significant that Bunny is so unhappy that he must escape reality by meditating and by repeating this motto that represents a loss of individuality.

Analysis

These chapters use individual characters to develop the theme of humans as machines. Patty Keene is described as being like "a new automobile, which hadn't even had its radio turned on yet," again linking humans to machines, specifically cars. She, like many women in Midland City, has become an agreeing machine instead of a thinking machine: "All their minds had to do was to discover what other people were thinking, and then they thought that, too." Here, Vonnegut uses the theme of humans as machines to demonstrate yet another common theme, the theme of ideas as disease. This rapid spreading of thoughts among "agreeing machines" clearly parallels the spreading of physical disease among bodies. The use of measurements (for example, penis size) to characterize human beings also enforces the idea of humans as machines. In this case, they are breeding machines: of course it is important how big a man's penis is and how wide a woman's hips are if they are seen as only machines for making babies. This idea is demonstrated again a bit later in the chapter, when we learn that Dwayne received a brochure for a penis-extender in the mail two months before. It offered him pornographic motion pictures, and the still photographs "caused the sex excitation center in Dwayne's brain to send nerve impulses down to an erection center in his spine." This very scientific approach to arousal enforces the view of humans as sex machines.

As Dwayne recalls what he saw inside the room labeled *Destructive Testing* at the headquarters of the Pontiac Division of General Motors, he wonders aloud, "if that was what God put me on Earth for - to find out how much a man could take without breaking." This anecdote demonstrates the theme of humans as machines, specifically as cars, once again. It also foreshadow's Dwayne's mental breakdown brought on by Trout's book that convinces him that he is the only human in the world. He feels very alone, as if God had a destructive plan for him, and thus it is easy for him to be pushed over the edge when Trout's written words speak to him.

Race is also very apparent in these chapters; when Patty Keene apologizes for her language, the narrator comments that black people in particular defied being taught correct English, and instead went on "talking English every *which* way." This draws attention to race, another common theme, and that language distinguishes race among humans as well as appearance. It also suggests that the narrator himself might be subject to racism. The worker at the construction site calls the machine Dwayne asks about "[The Hundred Nigger Machine]," referring to the time of slavery, when black people used to be treated as machines. This comment by a minor character not only likens humans to machines, it demonstrates how racism is embedded in the society in which Dwayne Hoover lives. The conversation between Harry LeSabre and his wife in which they use the code word "reindeer" to refer to their black maid, further demonstrates this idea. They often discuss the "reindeer problem," which is that black people reproduce like "useless, big black animals" and loiter around. Again, the theme of race emerges. Using this code word allows Harry and Grace to be racist without "giving offense to any black person who might overhear." This is extremely ironic, since their racism is extremely offensive in likening black people to an animal.

The conversation Trout has in Chapter 16 with the driver of the *Galaxie* hearkens back to the one between Trout and the driver of the Pyramid truck, in which that driver had the same answer for why a truck company would be named *Pyramid*. The theme of the advertising is linked to the way things sound, and it is significant to note that although the radio advertisements in the parking lot were "lullabies" to Dwayne Hoover's ears, Trout is for some reason unable to identify advertisements that work because of the way they sound. This is a key difference between the two men: Dwayne is susceptible to advertisements, while Trout is not, instead questioning their logic.

The narrator now reveals the plot of Trout's novel *Now It Can Be Told," which we as readers know through foreshadowing will cause Dwayne Hoover to go completely crazy. This story acts as a mirror, or "leak," reflecting Breakfast of Champions itself. The narrator is the Creator of the Universe, and Dwayne Hoover assumes that he is The Man. However, he lacks free will; the narrator often points out that the characters in his book have no power over what happens to them. This idea is reinforced by the foreshadowing technique Vonnegut employs to make sure we understand that the characters' fates are decided, from the very beginning of the story.*

Summary and Analysis of Chapters 18-19

Summary

Kilgore Trout is still a passenger in the *Galaxie*, stuck in traffic on the interstate. He passes a sign that says, "Turn Back! You have just passed Sacred Miracle Cave!"

Meanwhile, Dwayne Hoover is in the dark cocktail lounge of the new Holiday Inn. Bunny is playing the piano, but he and his father ignore each other: "They had not exchanged greetings for many years."

Francine Pefko is back at the Pontiac agency, catching up on work. Vonnegut once again uses the technique of foreshadowing by reminding the reader, "Dwayne would beat her up very soon." Wayne Hoobler is the only other person on the grounds; Vonnegut has the narrator foreshadow his fate as well: "Dwayne would try to beat him up, too, but Wayne was a genius at dodging blows." Francine is described as "pure machinery at the moment, a machine made of meat - a typing machine,a filing machine." This is her job, as a secretary, and Vonnegut hearkens back to the theme of humans as machines here.

Wayne Hoobler is observing his surroundings, idling around, not knowing where to go. He misses jail: the "papery voice" of the radio he used to listen to, the "clash of steel doors," the food, and the sex. The narrator suggests a tombstone for Wayne Hoobler, which reads: "Black Jailbird. He Adapted to What There Was to Adapt to."

We learn that Dwayne has good teeth, because of the dental program at the Adult Correctional Institution at Shepherdstown. He listens to the orders that a waitress calls to the bartender in the cocktail lounge of the new Holiday Inn: a "Black and White and water." The narrator tells us:

> Wayne should have pricked up his ears at that. That particular
> drink wasn't for any ordinary person. That drink was for the person
> who had created all Wayne's misery to date, who could kill him or
> make him a millionaire or send him back to prison or do whatever
> he damn pleased with Wayne. That drink was for me.

Now, Vonnegut uses the technique of direct address to completely breach the bounds between the universe of the narrator and that of the characters. The narrator is omniscient, as he describes himself above, but is now interacting with the world he controls, the world of the story. However, although Wayne Hoobler's fate is entirely in the narrator's hands, the next passage implies that the other characters have some amount of free will:

> I was there to watch a confrontation between two human beings I
> had created: Dwayne Hoover and Kilgore Trout.

The diction choice of the word "watch" suggests that some of the events which are to happen are not completely controlled by the narrator. Of course, he has planned them out, since he has been foreshadowing them for us throughout the story.

The narrator tells us the readers that he is wearing sunglasses so that he can be incognito. His sunglasses are important, because they embody the idea of mirrors as "leaks":

> The lenses were silvered, were mirrors to anyone looking my way. Anyone wanting to know what my eyes were like was confronted with his or her own twin reflections. Where other people in the cocktail lounge had eyes, I had two holes into another universe. I had *leaks*.

The narrator names his white cocktail waitress Bonnie MacMahon, and creates a life for her. She serves Dwayne Hoover a martini and says the same joke she says every time she serves a martini: "Breakfast of Champions." Dwayne hopes that he will meet some of the artists that are coming to the arts festival in the cocktail lounge. He hopes that they will reveal truths to him, and that these truths will "enable him to laugh at his troubles, to go on living, and to keep out of the North Wing of the Midland County General Hospital, which was for lunatics." Vonnegut uses dramatic irony here, since we as readers know, thanks to foreshadowing, that Dwayne's hopes are exactly the opposite of what is to be the actual result of his interactions with the artists.

As he waits, Dwayne recites a poem that he learned in school:

The Moving Finger writes; and, having writ,

Moves on: nor all your Piety nor Wit

Shall lure it back to cancel half the Line

Nor all your Tears wash out a Word of it.

The narrator sums up, "Some poem!" Dwayne becomes hypnotized by the poem and misses the entrance of Beatrice Keedsler, the Gothic novelist, and Rabo Karabekian, the minimal painter. Beatrice Keedsler and Rabo Karabekian have a conversation, in which they discuss how Midland City must be "the asshole of the Universe."

Meanwhile, Trout decides to get out of the *Galaxie* and walk, since it is stuck in traffic on the Interstate. He thinks about how to achieve "his narrow mission in Midland City, which was to show provincials, who were bent on exalting creativity, a would-be creator who had failed and failed." He examines himself in the rearview mirror, the *leak* of a truck with the message *Peerless* written in huge letters, twice, on it. His image in the *leak* is shocking: he is covered in blood and dog shit. The narrator points out that the dog from whom the shit came was "a wretched greyhound belonging to a girl I knew." The dog's name is Lancer, and his "entire life was devoted to unloading his excrement at the proper time and place." The inclusion of this detail about the dog's owner being someone the narrator knows takes another step toward doing away with the boundary between universes. How is it possible that the narrator should have an acquaintance within the universe he himself created?

Trout continues walking and discovers the cause of all the traffic on the interstate: a *Queen of the Prairies* milk truck has gotten into an accident with a Chevy, whose driver was lying dead in Sugar Creek. Coincidentally, *Queen of the Prairies* is the brand of milk that Wayne Hoobler used to drink in prison. "Milk and blood were about to be added to the composition of the stinking ping-pong balls which were being manufactured in the bowels of Sacred Miracle Cave." The pollution of Sugar Creek is thus entirely blamed on humans: the milk which they drink and the blood which they bleed are adding to the destruction of the environment.

Chapter 19 begins with the narrator affirming his role in the universe of his characters: "I was on a par with the Creator of the Universe there in the dark in the cocktail lounge." He plays with the universe, having it shrink and then explode. The narrator ponders the question of time, informing the reader that time is "a serpent which eats its tail," and providing a sketch of such a serpent. The snake "uncoiled itself long enough to offer Eve the apple," and we are provided with the second sketch of an apple so far in the story. The narrator tells us that the apple Eve and Adam ate was the Creator of the Universe, and states, "Symbols can be so beautiful, sometimes." This reflective statement is Vonnegut's self-conscious way of addressing all the symbols in the story so far. The reader is encouraged to acknowledge them for what they are.

The narrator has a conversation with the waitress, Bonnie MacMahon. He tells her that he can tell fortunes (which is, of course, true in her case) but she refuses his offer to have her fortune told. The narrator decides that the bartender is named Harold Newcomb Wilbur, and that is the second most decorated veteran in Midland City, after all the medals he won in World War II. The bartender is staring at the narrator, and the narrator wants him to stop. This prompts the narrator to describe his role:

> Here was the thing about my control over the characters I created: I could only guide their movements approximately, since they were such big animals. There was inertia to overcome. It wasn't as though I was connected to them by steel wires. It was more as thought I was connected to them by stale rubberbands.

This description hints at the role the creator of the reader's universe might play as well. It explains why the characters have some sort of free will, based upon the narrator's mood and will to participate.

In order to stop the bartender from staring at him, the narrator makes the phone ring, and makes Ned Lingamon be on the other line. He is the most decorated veteran in Midland City, beating even Harold Newcomb Wilbur, and he is jail for killing his own baby. The narrator confides that he could have told the fortunes of Bonnie MacMahon and of Bunny Hoover, and provides a summary for the reader's benefit.

Wayne Hoobler is standing outside the lounge among the garbage cans, looking at the money that had been given to him when he was let out of jail that morning. He sees a truck go by, and reads the message on its side: "Hertz." His reading the word hearkens back to the theme of advertising, and how a child would interpret it. Wayne Hoobler is, in terms of experiences, the most childlike main character in the story, but we know that Dwayne Hoover also experiences advertisements like a child, and that Trout plays a game in which he tries to see them through a child's eyes. The narrator reveals a bit about the near future of Wayne Hoobler.

Now we return to Rabo Karabekian and Beatrice Keedsler, who the narrator decides will "say and do some more stuff for the sake of this book." The narrator doodles on his tabletop with a damp fingertip. He draws the symbol for *nothingness*, which is an open circle, or a zero. He draws the sign for *everything*: an infinity loop. Then he writes out the word "Drano." Then he draws the sign for *pi*. Then he makes an "invisible duplicate" of Rabo Karabekian's painting entitled *The Temptation of Saint Anthony*. The original painting *The Temptation of Saint Anthony* is a 20x16 foot green wall with a vertical stripe of dayglo orange tape. Midland City, the narrator, and Beatrice Keedsler are all "outraged" that the painting had been the first purchase for the permanent collection of the Mildred Barry Memorial Center for the Arts, at $50,000. Karabekian is aware that everyone in the cocktail lounge hates him for "getting so much money for so little work," and he is amused. Beatrice Keedsler asks Karabekian who Saint Anthony was, and Karabekian himself doesn't know. The narrator confesses that he has "no respect whatsoever for the creative works of either the painter or the novelist."

The narrator explains that he pities Americans for trying to live like characters in storybooks. In this description, it is unclear whether it is the narrator or Vonnegut himself speaking, since the speaker confides that:

> Once I understood what was making America such a dangerous, unhappy nation of people who had nothing to do with real life, I resolved to shun storytelling. I would write about life. Every person would be exactly important as any other. All facts would also be given equal weightiness. Nothing would be left out. Let others bring order to chaos. I would bring chaos to order, instead, which I think I have done.

This passage describes the way *Breakfast of Champions* works, and explains why there are so many characters with individual stories and backgrounds. For that reason, the line between narrator and Vonnegut is blurred here: whose book is it?

Bonnie MacMahon brings Karabekian another martini, and they have a conversation about how she says "Breakfast of Champions" each time she brings any customer a martini. The narrator reveals to the reader who Saint Anthony actually was: an Egyptian who founded teh very first monastery. The Catholic high school in Midland City is named after Saint Anthony's biographer, Saint Athanasius.

Eldon Robbins, a black male dishwasher, steps outside for a cigarette. He recognizes Wayne Hoobler, since he too used to be an inmate at the Adult Correctional Institution, and he brings him inside and gives him a free steak and mashed potatoes and gravy and "anything else he wanted, all prepared by other black men in the kitchen." He shows Wayne a peephole through which he can look into the cocktail lounge and "watch the animals in the zoo." Wayne observes that Bonnie and Karabekian are still talking with each other.

Karabekian is making fun of Bonnie, teasing her by asking her to provide Beatrice Keedsler with details for her novels. Bonnie is deceived by his friendliness, and tells him the story of how her husband, who is a guard at the Shepherdstown Adult Correctional Institution, had to keep a white man named Leroy Joyce company before he was executed for his crime of rape. Leroy Joyce "was so dumb," that he cut off his penis and presented it to Bonnie's husband, as if now he wouldn't have to go to the electric chair after all. The narrator reveals that although "this story" itself is made up, the story of Leroy Joyce actually happened. In addition, Sparky is modeled after a real dog. This inclusion of "real" details in a story the narrator acknowledges as fictional further blurs the line between universes.

Karabekian asks Bonnie to tell him and Beatrice Keedsler something about Mary Alice Miller, the fifteen-year-old Women's Two Hundred Meter Breast Stroke Champion of the World, who is on the cover of the program for the Festival of the Arts. Bonnie tells the artist and novelist that Mary Alice's father taught her to swim when she was eight months old. Karabekian asks, "What kind of a man would turn his daughter into an outboard motor?" Now the narrator proclaims:

> And now comes the spiritual climax of this book, for it is at thsi
> point that I, the author, am suddenly transformed by what I have
> done so far. This is why I had gone to Midland City: to be born
> again.

The narrator describes the "pre-earthquake condition" of the "spiritual matrix of the cocktail lounge." That comment made by Karabekian was the force that upset the balance: "... a grain of sand crumbled. One force had a sudden advantage over another, and spiritual continents began to shrug and heave." One of the forces is the jealousy of the people in the cocktail lounge for Karabekian's sudden wealth due to his piece of art. Another force is their fear that "their lives might be ridiculous, that their entire city might be ridiculous." Karabekian has drawn attention to this fear by questioning their town's hero, Mary Alice Miller.

The narrator's own condition is described as:

> I had come to the conclusion that there was nothing sacred about
> myself or about any human being, that we were all machines,
> doomed to collide and collide and collide.

This realization on the narrator's part reinforces the image he drew of time as a
serpent eating its own tail. If he is just realizing this idea now, how have all the
references to humans as machines existed earlier in the story? The narrator is now
included in the theme of humans as machines, making him truly a character in his
own story.

Bonnie MacMahon explodes for the first time since she's been a waitress in the
cocktail lounge. She confronts Karabekian about his painting, saying she has "seen
better pictures done by a five-year-old." Karabekian responds to her criticism by
addressing "all those enemies" in the cocktail lounge, standing up. His description of
the painting is important:

> "I now give you my word of honor," he went on, "that the picture
> your city owns shows everything about life which truly matters,
> with nothing left out. It is a picture of the awareness of every
> animal. It is the immaterial core of every animal - the 'I am' to
> which all messages are sent. It is all that is alive in any of us - in a
> mouse, in a deer, in a cocktail waitress. It is unwavering and pure,
> no matter what preposterous adventure may befall us. A sacred
> picture of Saint Anthony alone is one vertical, unwavering band of
> light. If a cockroach were near him, or a cocktail waitress, the
> picture would show two such bands of light. Our awareness is all
> that is alive and maybe sacred in any of us. Everything else about
> us is dead machinery."

Analysis

Karabekian's speech contradicts the theme of humans as machines, or even animals
(as some humans are seen by others) as machines. That beam of consciousness
distinguishes us, readers in our universe, the narrator, and characters in his created
universe. It is significant, therefore, that Dwayne Hoover is still "hypnotized, turned
inward," and thus misses the speech. He is still susceptible to the message of *Now It
Can Be Told* by Kilgore Trout, which asserts that people are robots.

Wayne Hoobler's tombstone message hints at the theme of race, since we usually
think of animals as adapting to their environments. Black people throughout the story
have been compared to animals, and here Wayne Hoobler's entire existence is
summed up as one of adaptation. He misses what he knows, even though it is
captivity, much as an animal would. In fact, this passage links him to Trout's bird
Bill, who flew back into his cage because he was afraid of everything outside the

window. Vonnegut also uses Lancer the dog to reinforce the racial theme that black people are often seen as animals: he compares Lancer to Wayne Hoobler, because they both suspect that "some kind of terrible mistake had been made." In Chapter 19, when Eldon Robbins invites Wayne Hoobler to "watch the animals in the zoo," an important point is made about race. Up to this point it has been black people who are thought of as animals by white people. Now, the black kitchen staff is observing the white customers as if the white people are the animals.

The narrator's sunglasses make clear the purpose of Trout's calling mirrors "leaks" throughout the story. The narrator's sunglasses are truly leaks between universes: his own and that of the characters. He is able to watch his characters through the "leaks," but to the characters in their universe they are merely mirrors. As the narrator sits, he interacts with himself: he is truly a character within his created universe, as well as a being in the "real" universe, in which he exists without the characters of the story. He mouths the word *schizophrenia*, even though he is not certain he has this disease. By having the narrator mouth it, though, Vonnegut suggests that he in fact does suffer from the disease, and that affliction is what allows him to interact with this universe of his own creation. However, the narrator decides, "I am better now." This statement seems to come from a more recent reality, in which the narrator is looking back on the events of his interaction with his characters' universe, a time in which he was "really sick."

Vonnegut includes the poem Dwayne recites to himself to point out the power of the Creator of the Universe, in all universes. What has been decided by the narrator will happen to Hoover, and there is nothing he can do to change it; yet, the same is true for the narrator in the universe that Vonnegut has created. And the same is true for all of us, as readers, in whatever universe in which we happen to exist. However, the narrator's conversation with Bonnie MacMahon, and her subsequent conversation with the bartender, about which the narrator can only guess, reveals an important characteristic of the narrator: though he can, in fact, tell fortunes (and through foreshadowing has been doing so throughout the whole story), he is not in fact all-knowing, since he cannot guarantee that Bonnie MacMahon wants to have her fortune told, and does not know what her conversation with the bartender is about.

The narrator's confession that he has "no respect whatsoever for the creative works of either the painter or the novelist" (Karabekian and Keedsler) is important, and ironic, since the narrator himself is, within this work, both a painter and a novelist. The sketches we've seen throughout the story are apparently of his making, and of course *Breakfast of Champions* is a novel. Vonnegut has the narrator make this confession in order to reveal that perhaps the narrator himself is unaware of his own role; Vonnegut is the creator of *his* universe, and pulls the strings. However, a deep connection is implied between Vonnegut himself and the narrator, since the narrator now reveals that he is approaching his fiftieth birthday (the same is true for Vonnegut, as we learned in the introduction). The passage:

> And now comes the spiritual climax of this book, for it is at thsi point that I, the author, am suddenly transformed by what I have done so far. This is why I had gone to Midland City: to be born again.

confuses the narrator and Vonnegut himself, first of all by using the word "author." The narrator is supposedly the author of the universe of the book, but he himself is a character in the book written by Vonnegut. We know that *Breakfast of Champions* was a kind of rebirth for Vonnegut's career as a writer, and perhaps that is why he has created this alternate universe.

Summary and Analysis of Chapters 20-22

Summary

Kilgore Trout, who is walking the rest of the way to Midland City because of the traffic on the Interstate, reaches Sugar Creek and has to wade across. At once, his feet are coated in the clear, plastic substance that coats the surface of the creek. It comes from the Barrytron plant, which is manufacturing a new anti-personnel bomb for the Air Force and unknowingly polluting the creek with its waste. The Maritimo Brothers Construction Company, which is gangster-controlled, is supposed to be disposing of the waste in an effective way, but really it is just running a sewer pipe directly from Barrytron to Sugar Creek. Kilgore exits the stream and imagines entering the lobby of the new Holiday Inn, leaving wet footprints so someone will scold him. But he leaves no footprints because his feet are "sheathed in plastic and the plastic was dry." The narrator provides a sketch of the molecule that makes up plastic, accrediting it to Professor Walter H. Stockmayer of Dartmouth College, whom the narrator would like to be.

The narrator ties the plastic molecule with the indication of "etc." to the story itself, saying:

> The proper ending for any story about people it seems to me, since
> life is now a polymer in which the Earth is wrapped so tigtly,
> should be taht same abbreviation, which I now write large because
> I feel like it, which is this one (large drawing of the letters "ETC.")

> And it is in order to acknowledge the continuity of this polymer
> that I begin so many sentences with "And" and "So," and end so
> many paragraphs with "... and so on."

> And so on.

Trout stands in the lobby, surrounded by mirrors, which he calls *leaks*. The only other person in the lobby is the beautiful, young, homosexual desk clerk, Milo Maritimo, of the gangster family that is polluting Sugar Creek. Trout presents himself to Milo Maritimo, hoping to make an offensive impression, but Milo disappoints him by welcoming him grandiosely. Trout is absolutely bewildered by the fact that Milo knows who he is. Milo explains that when he couldn't find any information about Trout, he wrote to Eliot Rosewater, who let Milo read all the novels and short stories in his private collection. Milo is just finishing up the last one, *The Smart Bunny*. *The Smart Bunny* is about a rabbit who is as intelligent as Einstein or Shakespeare, and who is the only female leading character in any of Trout's work. She led a normal rabbit's life, and concluded that her intellect was useless, "that it was a sort of tumor, that it had no usefulness within the rabbit scheme of things." She is on her way to have the "tumor" removed when she is shot and killed. But the hunter who killed her and his wife decide she must be diseased because of her unusually large head, and don't eat her.

Milo Maritimo shows Trout to his suite, so he can change into his tuxedo right away. He implores Trout, "Oh, Mr. Trout... teach us to sing and dance and laugh and cry. We've tried to survive so long on money and sex and envy and real estate and football and basketball and automobiles and television and alcohol - on sawdust and broken glass!" Trout is outraged and tells Milo, "Open your eyes!" But Milo says his eyes *are* open, and he sees "a man who is terribly wounded - because he has dared to pass through the fires of truth to the other side, which we have never seen. And then he has come back again - to tell us about the other side."

Meanwhile, the narrator is still in the new Holiday Inn as well, making the building disappear and reappear again. He decides it is "high time" for Dwayne to meet Kilgore. The chapter ends with another bit of foreshadowing, when the narrator tells us:

> I knew how this book would end. Dwayne would hurt a lot of people. He would bite off one joint of the right index finger of Kilgore Trout.
>
> And then Trout, with his wound dressed, would walk out into the unfamiliar city. He would meet his Creator, who would explain everything.

Of course, the narrator is Trout's creator. So we know he has planned his own meeting with Trout.

Chapter 21 begins with Trout entering the cocktail lounge, with "fiery hot" feet since they are still coated in plastic, as well as in shoes and socks. He is once again anonymous, and nobody notices his entrance. Karabekian and Beatrice Keedsler are talking with "new affectionate" friends at the piano bar, since Karabekian's speech was so well-received. Dwayne is still in his own world, "mentally absent from activities in the cocktail lounge." He moves his lips, saying "Goodbye, Blue Monday" soundlessly. The narrator, Trout, and Hoover are being watched by Wayne Hoobler from the peephole in the kitchen. He is told to leave, and wanders back outdoors among the cars of the Pontiac agency.

The bartender flicks on the ultraviolet lights in the ceiling, and Bonnie MacMahon's uniform, the bartender's jacket, Bunny Hoover's smile, and other white things in the room are illuminated. Brightest of all is Kilgore Trout's new evening shirt, and its "beam was aimed at Dwayne Hoover." He comes out of his trance. Trout is "flabbergasted," since he knows nothing about science and cannot understand why all the white things in the room are lit up.

Dwayne "now lost himself in the bosom of Trout's shirt," and remembers for some reason "why there were no Niggers in Shepherdstown," something his stepfather had told him when he was ten years old. The two of them were on "a weekly expedition in the family car, hauling garbage and trash out into the country, where they dumped it all in Sugar Creek." According to the story Dwayne's stepfather had told him, black people were migrating north during the World War, and "there was such a labor shortage that even Niggers who couldn't read or write could get good factory jobs. Niggers had money like they never had before." However, the white people in Shepherdstown didn't want black neighbors, so they put up signs all over town reading: "Nigger! This is Shepherdstown. God Help You if the Sun Ever Sets on You Here!" One night, a black family got off a boxcar in Shepherdstown and disregarded the signs, staying in an empty shack. That night, a mob took out the man and "sawed him in two on the top strand of a barbed-wire fence."

Trout is uneasy because of how Dwayne is staring at him. He is also uneasy because of the narrator, since "Trout was the only character I ever created who had enough imagination to suspect that he might be the creation of another human being." It is embarrassing to him to be sitting so near his creator.

The narrator draws the equation "E=Mc^2" on the table, and thinks about how it is flawed since there is no "A" for *Awareness*, without which the other symbols could not exist. The theme of ownership appears with relation to this equation, when the narrator ponders how "the really smart people understood that one of the best ways to get rich was to own a part of the surface people had to stick to."

In order to avoid eye contact with Dwayne or the narrator, Trout sifts through the materials he has with him: the manilla envelope with his materials for the arts festival, which includes a letter from Fred T. Barry. The letter includes an explanation of how Barrytron was originally The Robo-Magic Corporation of America, and that the motto has remained the same: "Goodbye Blue Monday." Fred T. Barry wrote all the ads himself, including one of a black maid saying, "Feets, get movin'! Dey's got theirselves a Robo-Magic! Dey ain't gonna be needin' us 'rown' here no mo'!" This racist depiction was to advertise that eventually Robo-Magic appliances would do "all the Nigger work of the world, which was lifting and cleaning and cooking and washing and ironing and tending children and dealing with filth." Thus, the Robo-Magic and its motto, "Goodbye Blue Monday!" are inextricably linked to the theme of race. The narrator continues to expound upon this theme:

> I think that the end of the Civil War in my country frustrated the
> white people in the North, who won it, in a way which has never
> been acknowledged before. Their descendants inherited taht
> frustration, I think, without ever knowing what it was.

> The victors in that war were cheated out of the most desirable
> spoils of that war, which were human slaves.

This idea that the narrator has demonstrates his view that humans view each other as machines: even the Northern whites who won the war felt cheated because they didn't win the human machinery that should have been their "spoils."

The "brain" of the Robo-Magic later becomes the nerve center of the "BLINC System" or "Blast Interval Normalization Computer," during World War II, installed on bombers and completing the task of actually dropping the bombs after being directed to do so by the bombardier. It is fitting that this machine, which was the source of racism and perpetuated hatred in Midland City as the "brain" of the Robo-Magic, should cause death and destruction on a larger scale in a war.

At the beginning of Chapter 23, the narrator describes how he is wearing a bracelet that says, "WO1 Jon Sparks 3-19-71." WO1 stands for "Warrent Officer First Class," and this type of bracelet is becoming popular; wearers don't take them off until the prisoner of war whose name is on them is sent home. The narrator decides to leave the bracelet for Wayne Hoobler to find, since he won't know how to make sense of what is written on it.

The narrator decides also that Dwayne has taken a class in speed reading, in order to explain how he is able to read *Now It Can Be Told* in its entirety so quickly. Then the narrator takes a pill; mixed with the alcohol, it makes him feel that it is urgent to explain certain things he has not yet explained up to this point. For example, while in the hospital, Trout will see a jacket that says "Innocent Bystander H.S.," which has become the name of the high school originally named after Crispus Attucks.

The narrator also explains why so many black people in Midland City were able to imitate birds from the old British Empire. Fred T. Barry's family moved into the old Keedsler mansion, where Beatrice Keedsler grew up, and there were many black servants working for them. Fred T. Barry's mother could imitate birds from the British Empire, since she and her husband used to be music hall entertainers in England. All the black servants thought it was funny that she could imitate so many birds, so they learned how to, as well, and taught all their friends.

Dwayne's chemicals make him decide to accost Kilgore Trout in the cocktail lounge, and demand of him the secrets of life. He says, "Give me the message," and digs his chin into Trout's shoulder. The narrator explains that the Duchess does this to Alice in *Alice's Adventures in Wonderland*, and he's always wanted to have a character do this to another character. To get Dwayne to remove his chin from his shoulder, Trout gives him *Now It Can Be Told*, and Dwayne begins "to read hungrily."

Analysis

In Chapter 20, when Kilgore Trout's feet become coated in plastic, the pollution of Sugar Creek is evident in another way besides the ping-pong sized pollution bubbles taking over Lyle and Kyle Hoover's Sacred Miracle Cave. The pollution of the creek is tied to the theme of the destruction of the planet, and once again it is thanks to humans, in this case building ways to destroy each other. The plastic molecule is important to the story because Stockmayer indicated "points where it would go on and on" with the abbreviation "etc." This is an example of the narrator's self-conscious approach to the story.

In Chapter 21, Dwayne remembers the racist story his stepfather told him, when the two of them were on "a weekly expedition in the family car, hauling garbage and trash out into the country, where they dumped it all in Sugar Creek." The inclusion of this detail before recounting this very racist story is a way of connecting the theme of the destruction of the planet with the them of race. Dwayne's stepfather has been a racist character throughout the story, and it seems fitting that as he tells a story that Dwayne will remember his whole life, and which will come back to him right at the moment in which he goes completely crazy, they are polluting Sugar Creek. It is important that "Dwayne remembered clearly that a rainbow of oil from the trash was spreading prettily over the surface of Sugar Creek when he heard that." This imagery directly ties the pollution of the creek to this hate crime based on race. Humans' destruction of each other is thus linked to their destruction of the planet, at least in Dwayne's mind.

The fact that it is embarrassing for Trout to be sitting so close to his Creator, the narrator, is an important characteristic, since Trout himself is an author. He, unlike the narrator, seems aware that he is the character in a story, though they both write their *own* stories. This awareness is revealed through the character of Milo Maritimo, when Trout tells Milo, "Open your eyes!" But Milo says his eyes *are* open, and he sees "a man who is terribly wounded - because he has dared to pass through the fires of truth to the other side, which we have never seen. And then he has come back again - to tell us about the other side." It is interesting that the narrator points out this quality of awareness in Trout, though he himself cannot see that he is merely a character in Vonnegut's story.

In Chapter 21, there is an important description of the motto of The Robo-Magic Corporation of America, "Goodbye, Blue Monday," which is also the alternate title of *Breakfast of Champions*. It "cleverly confused two separate ideas people ahd about Monday," one being that Monday was washday, and not especially depressing. The other idea is that people with horrible jobs disliked Monday and called it "Blue Monday," but when Fred T. Barry made up the motto, he pretended that it was called "Blue Monday" because women hated doing the wash. The machine was going to "cheer them up." However, it is not true that women do the washing on Monday. When the Robo-Magic first came out, it had no competition, since it was during the Great Depression and nobody else could afford billboard space. "It was practically the only symbol in town." This detail reinforces the theme of advertising, and links the motto "Goodbye Blue Monday" to this theme, since it was at one point the only form of advertising in the town.

The fact that all black people in Midland City can imitate all birds from the old British Empire further links black people to animals, beyond just the connection of

Wayne Hoobler to caged birds. One of the birds they can imitate is the Bermuda Ern. They learn this skill from Fred T. Barry's mother, a wealthy white woman who employs them. So the thing that links them together as black people in Midland City was born from a racist institution.

Summary and Analysis of Chapters 23-24

Summary

Chapter 23 begins with Dwayne still reading *Now It Can Be Told*. He reads the following passage:

> "You are surrounded by loving machines, hating machines, greedy machines, unselfish machines, brave machines, cowardly machines, truthful machines, lying machines, funny machines, solemn machines," he read. "Their only purpose is to stir you up in every conceivable way, so the Creator of the Universe can watch your reactions. They can no more feel or reason than grandfather clocks."

The following paragraph that Dwayne reads references two other very important themes: the destruction of the planet and its overpopulation:

> "The Creator of the Universe would now like to apologize not only for the capricious, jostling companionship he provided during the tes, but for the trashy, stinking condition of the planet itself. The Creator programmed robots to abuse it for millions of years, so it would be a poisonous, festering cheese when you got here. Also, He made sure it would be desperately crowded by programming robots, regardless of their living conditions, to crave sexual intercourse and adore infants more than almost anything."

Mary Alice Miller walks through the cocktail lounge to get to the lobby to get a crown and scepter for her performance that night at the arts festival. Abe Cohen notices her and says out loud, "Pure tuna fish!" Kilgore Trout is unable to make sense of that exclamation. Meanwhile, his plastic-coated feet are getting very hot. Dwayne continues reading about how all other humans are robots "have committed every possible atrocity and every possible kindness unfeelingly, automatically, inevitably, to get a reaction from Y-O-U." The book continues to tell him about how his parents were machines of all types.

Now Dwayne gets up and walks over to the bar, "stiff" because of his "awe of his own strength and righteousness." He decides to "respond to his new understanding of life with finesse, for an audience of two - himself and his Creator." This phrasing is interesting, because his Creator is sitting right there - the narrator. So technically, Dwayne could also attack him, as a character within his own story. But instead he approaches Bunny, who responds by meditating and seeing the "phosphorescent scarf" float by in his mind, reading the word "Cool." Dwayne attacks his son, calling him a "God damn cock-sucking machine!" This diction choice once again draws attention to the theme of humans as machines. He slams Bunny's head over and over on the piano keys, and Bunny doesn't resist.

When Rabo Karabekian, Beatrice Keedsler, and Bonnie MacMahon pull him off his son, Dwayne punches Beatrice Keedsler in the jaw, and punches Bonnie MacMahon in the belly. He shouts, "All you robots want to know why my wife at Drano? I'll tell you why: She was that kind of machine!" This climactic scene really enforces the narrator's understanding of all humans as machines, through the character of Dwayne. Dwayne runs outside, where Mary Alice Miller's father, Don Miller, is waiting for her in the car. He is lying with his seat back flat, staring at the ceiling and trying to learn French on audio tape.

Dwayne calls "for Niggers to come talk to him," but when none come, he thinks that the Creator of the Universe has made them all hide as a joke. As the sun goes down, he calls out, "Olly-olly-ox-in-freeeeeeeeeee." Wayne Hoobler responds, though he has never played hide and seek in his life. He stands at *parade rest*, "ready for anything, and wouldn't mind death." Dwayne begins talking to him about all the black people he's ever known, and about his wife and son. Then Dwayne attempts to hit Wayne, but Wayne is extremely good at ducking; Dwayne calls him "African dodger!" Thinking that he is involved in a game of African dodger (in which a black man would stick his head through a hole at a carnival booth, while people paid to through baseballs at his head and won a prize if they hit him), Dwayne continues to try to attack Wayne. Wayne vaults up onto the bed of a truck, and Dwayne decides not to follow him up, saying, "You're too good for me." Then he continues talking to Wayne, now about human slavery. He includes not only black slaves, but coal miners and factory workers as well.

Wayne Hoobler's mouth falls open as he sees the runway lights of the nearby airport light up. To him, they look like his dream come true: they look like his childish idea of "Fairy Land."

In Chapter 24, Dwayne Hoover has injured so many people that *The Martha Simmons Memorial Mobile Disaster Unit* needs to be used, a special ambulance that is a full-sized transcontinental bus. It is named after the wife of Newbolt Simmons, who died of rabies after being bitten by a bat she was trying to save. Newbolt Simmons and Dwayne were "drawn together for a while," because their wifes had died strange deaths within a month of each other. Their friendship petered out, but they still exchanged Christmas cards (drawings are provided of each card).

The narrator tells us that his psychiatrist is also named Martha. He decides that rather than the American novelist Thomas Wolfe's idea of keeping the search for a father in mind as a unifying idea in writing, heroes and heroines ought to be searching for mothers instead. He draws attention to how both Dwayne Hoover and Wayne Hoobler are motherless. We learn how Eliot Rosewater killed his mother accidentally in a boating accident. The pilot of his plane, Colonel Looseleaf Harper, causes the runway of the Will Fairchild Memorial Airport to light up, looking like Fairyland to Wayne Hoobler. The narrator reminds us of his role as Creator of the

Universe, at least of the universe of the characters, by pointing out, "I could have killed him, and his pilot, too, but I let them live on. So their plane touched down uneventfully."

Back on *Martha* the disaster vehicle, Cyprian Ukwende and Khashdrahr Miasma are the physicians in charge. Eddie Key is the name of the driver, and is the direct descendant of Francis Scott Key, who wrote the National Anthem. Eddie is black, and can name more than six hundred of his ancestors, who are Africans, Indians and white men. His ancestors owned "Bluebird Farm," which was the "Nigger Farm" where Dwayne Hoover's stepfather discovered Sacred Miracle Cave. As he drives the vehicle, "he had the feeling that he himself was a vehicle, and that his eyes were windshields through which his progenitors could look, if they wished to."

Dwayne is boarded into *Martha*, believing his is on the virgin planet of *Now It Can Be Told*. He believes that he is The Man of the story, yelling out phrases of his own free will, which the Creator of the Universe cannot guess. He yells, "Goodbye, Blue Monday!" As Kilgore Trout climbs into *Martha*, we learn that he had jumped Dwayne from behind when Dwayne dragged Francine Pefko out onto the asphalt to give her a beating in public. He had broken her jaw and three ribs inside the office. Now she is unconscious and the most seriously injured victim. When Trout grabbed Dwayne from behind, somehow his right ring finger slipped into Dwayne's mouth, and Dwayne bit it off from the topmost joint. He spat it into Sugar Creek.

Wayne Hoobler remained unhurt, and is now among the cars on the Pontiac lot, finding the bracelet the narrator had tossed there for him. But the narrator himself is injured in the scuffle: "I came out of the riot with a broken watch crystal and what turned out later to be a broken toe. Somebody jumped backwards to get out of Dwayne's way. He broke my watch crystal, even though I had created him, and he broke my toe." The only person whom Dwayne hurt who deserved it was Don Breedlove. He had been repairing a defective gas oven in the kitchen of the new Holiday Inn. Dwayne had once sold Breedlove a Pontiac *Ventura*, and Breedlove had written "This Car is a Lemon!" all over it. Dwayne offers Breedlove his hand, and they shake; while Breedlove is led to believe Dwayne is making a motion of friendship, Dwayne boxes him in the ear, causing him to go deaf.

Cyprian Ukwende tries to remove Dwayne Hoover's shoes, but they are plasticized because he has waded across Sugar Creek. He asks Dr. Khashdrahr Miasma to get some shears so he can cut them off, but Miasma refuses, and is altogether unhelpful.

The narrator now says, "I could go on and on with the intimate details about the various lives of people on the super-ambulance, but what good is more information?" Earlier he told us that he wants to write about life, since writing fictitious novels negatively affects real people who try to live their lives like characters in a story book. However, now he relates to another of Kilgore Trout's novels, *The Pan-Galactic Memory Bank*, in which the hero gets a realistic novel out of a library, reads about sixty pages of it, then takes it back saying, "I already know about human beings."

Dwayne Hoover momentarily regains sanity, and speaks to Cyprian Ukwende about opening a health club in Midland City. But the narrator tells us his fortune, which is that "He wasn't going to open anything ever again." His victims will sue him for all he is worth, and he will become "one more withered balloon of an old man on Midland City's Skid Row." This points out the idea that all humans are characters of equal weight; although this whole story has been written about the most catastrophic point in Dwayne Hoover's life, to passersby later he will just be a random homeless man.

Analysis

The passage that Dwayne reads from *Now It Can Be Told* in the beginning of Chapter 23 sums up the theme of humans as machines and what we know from foreshadowing is the idea that drives him over the brink of insanity. As Dwayne rants to Wayne Hoobler in the parking lot, he acknowledges that "white robots were just like black robots, essentially, in that they were programmed to be whatever they were, to do whatever they did." This conclusion Dwayne reaches in his madness reconciles the idea of humans as machines with the theme of race. Thinking of humans as machines allows them all to be equal, regardless of race. Dwayne concludes that nothing is really a shame, since "Why should I care what happens to machines?" This rationale could be used to justify any type of injustice, as it already has for Dwayne: he is attacking people on his rampage because he doesn't believe they can feel anything.

In Chapter 24, the narrator seems to act as a reader of his own story, pointing out the theme of motherlessness. The narrator's pointing out his own themes demonstrates Vonnegut's destruction of barriers between universes; the narrator is a character in his created universe, but also comments on themes that permeate it. The narrator's injury in Dwayne's rampage is significant because it totally defies the laws of separate universes; we already saw the narrator observe his characters through "leaks," and even interact with them, but now he is physically injured during the time he spends in their universe.

The character of Eddie Key is extremely instrumental in tying the theme of race up to the theme of America inextricably here, since Eddie is black, and can name more than six hundred of his ancestors, who are Africans, Indians and white men. His ancestors owned "Bluebird Farm," which was the "Nigger Farm" where Dwayne Hoover's stepfather discovered Sacred Miracle Cave. It is significant that Eddie Key is driving the ambulance with all the victims of Dwayne's insanity inside. Because of his mixed ancestry, he represents a cross section of America, and as he drives the vehicle, "he had the feeling that he himself was a vehicle, and that his eyes were windshields through which his progenitors could look, if they wished to." Since Eddie Key envisions himself as a machine, specifically a car, we make the connection that all Americans are machines; this connection is emphasized when

"Eddie focused his eyes on an American flag which was stuck to the windshield. He said this very quietly: 'Still wavin', man.'" This line is a beacon of hope; perhaps the only clear one in the whole story. Despite all the destruction in the very vehicle he is driving, Eddie Key feels himself to be a vehicle through which history continues to be made, building upon itself through generations of Americans.

"Goodbye, Blue Monday!" returns in its final incarnation as Dwayne is loaded into *Martha*. He believes that he is The Man of the story, yelling out phrases of his own free will, which the Creator of the Universe cannot guess. He yells, "Goodbye, Blue Monday!" The return of this phrase implies something important about themes throughout this story. After all the meanings suggested and heaped upon this phrase throughout the story, as it turns out, it is entirely random. Dwayne yells it because of his free will, but it also represents his insanity.

It is significant also that Dwayne spat Trout's severed finger into Sugar Creek. Thus Sugar Creek has become more polluted with human waste; in this case, a severed body part. As Trout walked along the Interstate on his way to Midland City, he had observed an accident in which milk and blood were pouring into Sugar Creek; now his finger joins them in its pollution. This draws attention to the theme of the destruction of the Earth; humans' insanity and destruction of themselves, in this case that of Dwayne Hoover, but also in the case of the automobile accident, is causing it.

Summary and Analysis of Epilogue

Summary

After Kilgore Trout's finger is treated, he gets lost in the basement where the emergency room is located. He is "destitute," with no health insurance or cash. As he wanders past the morgue and the x-ray room, he "automatically mooned about his own mortality." He passes the room of Elgin Washington, a young, "fabulously well-to-do" pimp who operated out of the old Holiday Inn. Khashdrahr Miasma has amputated his foot, perhaps unnecessarily, earlier in the day, and now Elgin has just sniffed cocaine. Elgin wants to make Trout feel diminished, as he does with everyone. He tells him, "I think I may be dying." Then he asks him to listen to him as he imitates the Nightingale. This is a reminder of the talent all black people in Midland City share: imitating birds.

The Midland City Festival of the Arts has been postponed, but Trout has not been informed because he had wandered away by the time Fred T. Barry came to the hospital to tell him. Now he is walking back down Fairchild Boulevard, and the narrator is waiting to intercept him smoking a cigarette. When he gets out of his Plymouth *Duster*, he tells us, "I feared nothing. That was foolish of me." This is surprising, since he is in a world of his own creation. However, he is about to be attacked by a Doberman pinscher named Kazak. Kazak was taken care of by the husband of Lottie Davis, Dwayne Hoover's maid, and abused and then turned loose. He looks at the old Keedsler mansion, where Beatrice Keedsler had been raised, and where her uncle had committed the murder of five relatives, three servants, two policemen, and all the animals in their private zoo because of a brain tumor. Then the mansion was inhabited by Fred T. Barry's family, and now it belongs to the city. Fred T. Barry wants to make it into a museum, as long as it exhibits the first *Robo-Magic* and explains "how machines evolved just as animals did, but with much greater speed." When the narrator is attacked by Kazak, his testicles also retracted into his abdominal cavity, and he is told he'll need surgery to bring them down.

Trout still approaches, and now he sees the narrator, his Creator, leap completely over an automobile and land on his hands and knees in the middle of the street. Kazak is knocked silly when he is stopped by the fence. Trout turns around and starts to run away, but the narrator chases him in his car. Kilgore stops running when the narrator calls him by name, in front of the General Electric Company. The monogram and motto read, "Progress is our most important product." This motto hearkens back to the theme of advertising, now tying it to the idea that has just been introduced of machines evolving like living things. General Motors products are making "progress," just as the *Robo-Magic* evolved.

Now the narrator attempts to turn on the dome light in his car, to let Trout have a look at him. However, he is unable to control the machine that is his automobile just as he is unable to control the machine-characters in his created universe:

I thought it would be a good idea to let him have a good look at me, and so attempted to flick on the dome light. I turned on the windshield wipers instead. I turned them off again. My view of the lights of the County Hospital was garbled by beads of water. I pulled at another switch, and it came away in my hand. It was a cigarette lighter. So I had no choice but to continue to speak from darkness.

The narrator tells Trout, "I'm your Creator. You're in the middle of a book right now - close to the end of it, actually." He tells Trout that he is going to win a Nobel Prize, and have a reputable publisher. All Trout wants to ask him is, "Do you have a gun?" And then, "Are you *crazy*?" To prove that he is not crazy, the narrator transports him all over the world: to the Taj Mahal, Venice, Dar es Salaam, the surface of the Sun, to the Bermuda of his childhood, and to the Indianapolis of the narrator's childhood. This demonstration of power enforces the idea that the narrator himself is a character, since it links him to Trout by making Trout share his formative experience of seeing a man with *locomotor ataxia*, acting like a machine.

The narrator now noisily gets out of his car and tells Trout that he is holding something in his hand, even though there is nothing there. Such is his power over Trout that he will see whatever the narrator wants him to. The narrator says,

> "I hold in my hand a symbol of wholeness and harmony and nourishment. It is Oriental in its simplicity, but we are *Americans*, Kilgore, and not Chinamen. We Americans require symbols which are richly colored and three-dimensional and juicy. Most of all, we hunger for symbols which have not been poisoned by graet sins our nation has committed, such as slavery and genocide and criminal neglect, or by tinhorn commercial greed and cunning."

Trout looks up and sees that the author is holding an apple in his hand. This is significant because an apple is one of the most important symbols in literature (stemming from the story of Adam and Eve in Genesis in the Bible), and it has been a kind of symbol throughout this story: the narrator has drawn two pictures of it. But it is rendered meaningless by the words the narrator has just said to Trout.

The narrator tells Trout that as he approaches his fiftieth birthday, he is going to set all his characters free. Then he says "Bon voyage" and "somersaulted lazily and pleasantly through the void, which is my hiding place when I dematerialize." A small hand mirror floats by the narrator as he travels between universes. It is another symbol, a *leak* between universes, very obviously heralding the narrator's departure from the universe of the characters. Trout's voice is the narrator's father's voice as he yells, "Make me young, make me young, make me young!"

Analysis

As Trout wanders past the morgue and x-ray room, the narrator uses the opportunity to again remind us of his opinion that humans are machines: "Trout felt nothing now that millions of other people wouldn't have felt - automatically." Even as Trout experiences the most aware, seemingly human feelings of questioning one's mortality, he is acting in accordance with his machinery. This comparison suggests that despite Karabekian's speech about his painting and how it represents awareness, which distinguishes living things from inanimate objects, the narrator has not been convinced.

As the narrator ponders his surroundings before being attacked by Kazak, he has become *completely* a character in his own created universe, as he tells us, "I should have known that a character as ferocious as Kazak was not easily cut out of a novel." But he is unaware as he looks at the old Keedsler Mansion. We have already seen that as long as he physically exists in the universe of his own creation, he is vulnerable: he was accidentally injured during Dwayne's rampage, and now, supposedly, has a broken toe.

The fact that Fred T. Barry wants to make the old Keedsler mansion into a museum that shows "how machines evolved just as animals did, but with much greater speed" is interesting, since this idea reverses the them of humans as machines and instead gives machines the living quality of evolution. The theme of humans as machines is demonstrated explicitly in Kazak's attack of the narrator. The narrator's response to the attack is described purely in scientific terms rather than emotional ones: "Everything my body had done so far fell within normal operating procedures for a human machine."

The scene in which the narrator tries to turn on his dome light in the car so that Trout can see him more clearly is significant. It is an allegory for the Creator of the *narrator's* universe, as well as that of the *reader*. The car, in addition to Trout himself, is a metaphor for the Creator's characters; this metaphor has been built up throughout the story by the theme of humans as machines. It seems to have its own free will as the narrator tries to control it, in order to reveal himself as Creator to Trout.

What the narrator says to Trout about symbols suggests that any symbolism the reader has found in the story is merely the creation of the reader, searching for meaning. This is assuming the reader is American, since this search for symbols is described as a uniquely American quality. An example we have seen of this is the symbol "Goodbye, Blue Monday," which, despite all the meanings heaped upon it throughout the story, has been demonstrated to be empty after all, when Dwayne Hoover shouts it out randomly in the ambulance. The "tinhorn commercial greed and cunning" refers to the theme of advertising, which has permeated the story.

Suggested Essay Questions

1. **In your opinion, is the narrator racist?**

   Race is certainly a central theme of *Breakfast of Champions*, but it is debatable whether the narrator himself holds racist views. He points out the racist views of certain characters, for instance Dwayne's stepfather. The advertising campaign for the original *Robo-Magic* also demonstrates a widespread racism, drawing upon the audience's conception of washing and other menial tasks as "Nigger work." Debate whether there is a distinction between the narrator's point of view and that he confers upon his characters and Americans in general as represented in the text.

2. **What is the relationship between the narrator and Vonnegut himself?**

   From what we as readers know about Vonnegut, he has a lot in common with the narrator: for instance, their mothers committed suicide and they are approaching their fiftieth birthdays. These similarities suggest that the narrator might represent Vonnegut, seen through a mirror, or "leak" into another universe. But the narrator interacts with his characters and becomes a character himself, with opinions and ideas designated to him by Vonnegut, the author. Address passages in which the narrator uses the direct address technique to analyze to what extent he represents Vonnegut himself, and to what extent Vonnegut makes him into a character.

3. **Why, after the narrator says the following quotation, does Trout see an apple in his hand?**

   > "I hold in my hand a symbol of wholeness and harmony and nourishment. It is Oriental in its simplicity, but we are *Americans*, Kilgore, and not Chinamen. We Americans require symbols which are richly colored and three-dimensional and juicy. Most of all, we hunger for symbols which have not been poisoned by graet sins our nation has committed, such as slavery and genocide and criminal neglect, or by tinhorn commercial greed and cunning."

   An apple is a fitting image, it is in fact "richly colored and three-dimensional and juicy." It has also come to be a symbol of the United States, associated with Johnny Appleseed and Apple pie, as wholesome. There have been two drawings of apples throughout the story; it has in fact, been made into a symbol by the narrator. But the above passage suggests that it is only a symbol because of the meaning Americans endow it with, not because of any inherent quality in the apple itself.

4. **How are black people characterized as animals?**

When we are introduced to Wayne Hoobler, he feels as though he's free for the first time in his life, since he has always been kept in "orphanages and youth shelters and prisons of one sort or another." He misses prison, since now that he is free he doesn't know what to do with himself. This is similar to what happened to Bill, Trout's bird, when he freed it from its cage and it decided to hop back inside because it was afraid of what was beyond the window. He believes that the planet is terrible, and feels like he doesn't belong on it since he has no friends or relatives, and is always being put in cages. This sense is similar to the feelings of Kazak, the dog who attacks the narrator in the Epilogue.

All the black people in Midland City also know how to imitate birds, thanks to Fred T. Barry's mother. This links them all to each other, as well as to animals in that they are being oppressed and struggling against white people (in the case of birds, like the now extinct Bermuda Ern, against humans in general).

5. **Discuss the significance of the phrase "Goodbye, Blue Monday."**

This is the alternate title of the book, as well as the motto of the company which Dwayne Hoover was able to sell in order to buy the Pontiac agency. The company advertised the *Robo-Magic* in a racist campaign, and its motto was "practically the only symbol in town." It is also the phrase that Dwayne Hoover yells out in the ambulance when he thinks he is The Man, the protagonist of Trout's story *Now It Can Be Told*, using his free will to surprise the Creator of the Universe. Dwayne Hoover mouths it to himself as he zones out in the cocktail lounge immediately preceding his rampage. All the meaning heaped upon this symbolic phrase is challenged, though, by the narrator's speech to Trout in the Epilogue, in which he points out Americans' need for symbolism.

6. **How is an apple used as a self-aware symbol?**

There are two drawings of an apple, making it a literal symbol. One is when the narrator discusses how the the atmosphere of the Earth is as thin as the skin of an apple, and the other is after the narrator characterizes time as "a serpent which eats its tail." He draws the apple offered to Eve by the serpent, and says that the apple Eve ate was the Creator of the Universe, then says, "Symbols can be so beautiful sometimes." When the narrator accosts Trout in the Epilogue, Trout sees an apple in the narrator's hand, symbolizing American's need for symbolism.

7. **What is the purpose served by the inclusion of dogs as characters?**

Sparky is Dwayne Hoover's Labrador retriever, who cannot wag his tail and so has to fight other dogs all the time. Lancer is the dog whose excrement got on Trout when he was beaten up and left on the handball court, who has "a very small brain, but he must have suspected from time to time, just as Wayne Hoobler did, that some kind of terrible mistake had been made."

Kazak is the Doberman pinscher who attempts to attack the narrator in the Epilogue, who has been kept in a cage and beaten, and taught that his entire existence is to kill. These dogs exist as characters to be compared to the animal-like qualities of the human characters.

8. **The narrator believes Americans are doing their best to live like characters in story books, and decides to write about life. Discuss his attempt.**

The universe of the narrator's characters in *Breakfast of Champions* is apparently his attempt at writing about life; the universe which includes the narrator himself as a character can be seen as Vonnegut's attempt at the same. While many characters' lives are detailed beyond the status of minor character, it is untrue that each of them is equally important: obviously Dwayne and Kilgore are the protagonists. However, in including the details of individual characters' personal stories, whether they are consequential to the plot or not, Vonnegut "brings chaos to order" through the narrator.

9. **What is the significance of Karabekian's painting?**

Karabekian's painting, *The Temptation of Saint Anthony*, is resented at first by everyone in Midland City because it was purchased for $50,000 and could have been made by a five-year-old, according to Bonnie MacMahon. However, he defends it in Chapter 19 by saying that it "shows everything about life which truly matters, with nothing left out." It represents awareness, which all living things possess, as an unwavering band of light. This idea is a foil to the theme of humans as machines that has been developed throughout the story, since machines lack awareness.

10. **Discuss the significance of Eddie Key, calling upon the themes associated with America throughout the story.**

Eddie Key is a character in Chapter 24, the driver of *Martha* the emergency vehicle. His diverse ancestry, including Francis Scott Key, represents a cross-section of America. He imagines that his ancestors can look out of his eyes, as if they were leaks, as if he himself were a vehicle. He is the only clear symbol of hope in this story, as he focuses his eyes so that Francis Scott Key can see the American flag stuck to the windshield and says, "Still wavin', man." This hopeful phrase is in contrast to the negative light in which America is represented throughout the story, including commentaries on advertisement and ownership.

Quotations

"We are healthy only to the extent that our ideas are humane."

This is the epitaph on the monument built for Trout after he died. It is "a quotation from his last novel, his two-hundred-and-ninth novel, which was unfinished when he died." After Dwayne Hoover went to the asylum, Trout became obsessed with the with the notion that ideas can cause disease, as well as cure it. At first he was just "a dirty old man," but soon his ideas were taken seriously by artists and scientists alike.

"What is the purpose of life?"

Trout sees this message written on the tiled wall of the pornographic movie house on Forty-Second Street. He cannot write a response because he has no writing utensil, but wants to write:

> "To be the eyes and ears and conscience of the Creator of the Universe, you fool."

"Everything you're not supposed to do to a car, they did to a car."

Dwayne says this while telling Francine about a trip he made to the headquarters of the Pontiac Division of General Motors, three months after his wife's suicide. He had witnessed the destruction of Pontiacs by scientists. The sign on the door read, Destructive Testing. Dwayne wonders aloud, "if that was what God put me on Earth for - to find out how much a man could take without breaking." This anecdote further underlines the theme of humans as machines, specifically as cars, once again. It also foreshadows Dwayne's mental breakdown brought on by Trout's book that convinces him that he is the only human in the world. He feels very alone, as if God had a destructive plan for him, and thus it is easy for him to be pushed over the edge when Trout's written words speak to him.

"Wayne should have pricked up his ears at that. That particular drink wasn't for any ordinary person. That drink was for the person who had created all Wayne's misery to date, who could kill him or make him a millionaire or send him back to prison or do whatever he damn pleased with Wayne. That drink was for me."

This passage occurs in the cocktail lounge of the new Holiday Inn, when Wayne Hoobler overhears the narrator order a drink. It introduces the narrator's full involvement as a character in his own created universe. We as readers see mirrors acting as "leaks" in the form of the narrator's reflective sunglasses, as he watches his characters interact and controls them to the extent that he can.

"Still wavin', man."

Eddie Key says this very quietly as he drives *Martha* the emergency vehicle filled with Dwayne Hoover and all his victims. He focuses his eyes on an American flag stuck to the windshield, and says this quotation for the benefit of his ancestor, Francis Scott Key. This line is a beacon of hope; perhaps the only clear one in the whole story. Despite all the destruction in the very vehicle he is driving, Eddie Key feels himself to be a vehicle through which history continues to be made, building upon itself through generations of Americans.

"Trout felt nothing now that millions of other people wouldn't have felt - automatically."

This quotation is from the Epilogue, as Trout wanders past the morgue and the x-ray room, and "automatically mooned about his own mortality." The narrator uses this opportunity to again remind us of his opinion that humans are machines: Even as Trout experiences the most aware, seemingly human feelings of questioning one's mortality, he is acting in accordance with his machinery.

"I thought it would be a good idea to let him have a good look at me, and so attempted to flick on the dome light. I turned on the windshield wipers instead. I turned them off again. My view of the lights of the County Hospital was garbled by beads of water. I pulled at another switch, and it came away in my hand. It was a cigarette lighter. So I had no choice but to continue to speak from darkness."

The narrator attempts to turn on the dome light in his car, to let Trout have a look at him. However, he is unable to control the machine that is his automobile just as he is unable to control the machine-characters in his created universe. This scene is significant because it is an allegory for the Creator of the *narrator's* universe, as well as that of the *reader*. The car, in addition to Trout himself, is a metaphor for the Creator's characters; this metaphor has been built up throughout the story by the theme of humans as machines. It seems to have its own free will as the narrator tries to control it, in order to reveal himself as Creator to Trout.

"I hold in my hand a symbol of wholeness and harmony and nourishment. It is Oriental in its simplicity, but we are *Americans*, Kilgore, and not Chinamen. We Americans require symbols which are richly colored and three-dimensional and juicy. Most of all, we hunger for symbols which have not been poisoned by great sins our nation has committed, such as slavery and genocide and criminal neglect, or by tinhorn commercial greed and cunning."

The narrator says this to Trout in the Epilogue, after noisily getting out of his car. He tells Trout that he is holding something in his hand, even though there is nothing there; such is his power over Trout that he will see whatever the narrator wants him to. Eventually, Trout sees an apple; fittingly, since an apple is in fact "richly colored and three-dimensional and juicy," and has come to represent the United States.

This quotation suggests that any symbolism the reader has found in the story is merely the creation of the reader, searching for meaning. This is assuming the reader is American, since this search for symbols is described as a uniquely American quality. An example we have seen of this is the symbol "Goodbye, Blue Monday," which, despite all the meanings heaped upon it throughout the story, has been demonstrated to be empty after all, when Dwayne Hoover shouts it out randomly in the ambulance. The "tinhorn commercial greed and cunning" refers to the theme of advertising, which has permeated the story.

Kilgore Trout, a Recurring Character

Kilgore Trout is a recurring character in the Kurt Vonnegut canon. He is mentioned in *God Bless You, Mr. Rosewater*, which tells the story of Eliot Rosewater (the millionaire fan who writes Trout's only fan mail letter in *Breakfast of Champions*); he is featured in *Slaughterhouse-Five* as not only a failed science-fiction writer, but a manager of newsboys; he is the main character of *Timequake*. (Unlike the characters in the short stories that make up this last book, he is unaffected by the depression caused by watching oneself make bad decisions. Therefore, he is able to remain apathetic and help those who *are* affected by saying, "You were sick, now you're better, there's work to be done.")

He is mentioned in *Jailbird*, written in the style of a memoir about Walter F. Starbuck, who has just been released from prison for a minor involvement in the Watergate scandal. Trout is portrayed as the only American convicted of treason during the Korean war, and also the only prisoner serving a life sentence at the Federal Minimum Security Adult Correctional Facility near Finletter Air Force Base, Georgia.

Though Trout himself is not a character in *Galapagos*, his son Leon is the narrator (and, incidentally, dead). Leon mentions some of his father's stories, and provides summaries.

Kilgore Trout, a Recurring Character

Author of ClassicNote and Sources

Meghan Joyce, author of ClassicNote. Completed on November 15, 2008, copyright held by GradeSaver.

Updated and revised Damien Chazelle November 30, 2008. Copyright held by GradeSaver.

Thomas F. Marvin. Kurt Vonnegut: A Critical Companion. Westport, CT: Greenwood Publishing Group, 2002.

Jerome Klinkowitz. The Vonnegut Effect. Columbia, SC: University of South Carolina Press, 2004.

Lawrence R. Broer. Sanity Plea: Schizophrenia in the Novels of Kurt Vonnegut. Tuscaloosa, AL: University of Alabama Press, 1994.

Christopher Lehmann-Haupt. ""Is Kurt Vonnegut Kidding Us?"." Books of the Times. 1973-05-02. 2008-11-04. <http://nytimes.com/books>.

Chris Huber. "Kurt Vonnegut: His Life and Work." 2005-02-05. 2008-10-24. <http://www.vonnegutweb.com>.

Merill, Robert. "Vonnegut's 'Breakfast of Champions': The Conversion of Heliogabalus." *Modern Fiction* Vol.XVIII, No.3, pp. 99-108. 1977.

McGinnis, Wayne. "Vonnegut's Breakfast of Champions: A Reductive Success." *Notes on Contemporary Literature 5*. 1975. pp. 6-9.

Quiz 1

1. **What is Kilgore Trout's profession that makes him famous?**
   A. Janitor
   B. Science-fiction writer
   C. Garbage Man
   D. Businessman

2. **What is Dwayne Hoover's profession?**
   A. Business owner
   B. Cocktail waiter
   C. Science-fiction writer
   D. Piano player

3. **Who runs the Sacred Miracle Cave?**
   A. Kilgore Trout
   ʚ. Bonnie MacMahon
   C. Lyle and Kyle Hoover
   D. Bunny Hoover

4. **What is the term used to describe what many Americans own?**
   A. Doodley-squat
   B. Nada
   C. Zero
   D. Zilch

5. **Where are Trout's stories published?**
   A. On the backs of other novels
   B. In his backyard
   C. Random House
   D. Pornographic literature

6. **Who wins the Nobel Peace Prize?**
   A. Don Breedlove
   B. Dwayne Hoover
   C. Kilgore Trout
   D. Beatrice Keedsler

7. Which of the following is a millionaire?
A. Don Breedlove
B. Wayne Hoobler
C. Francine Pefko
D. Eliot Rosewater

8. What does the letter that Trout receives from Eliot Rosewater say?
A. That they are brothers
B. That he is invited to the arts festival
C. It is a death threat
D. That he should be President

9. Which character looks like a "Chinaman"?
A. Dwayne's stepfather
B. Kilgore Trout
C. Fred T. Barry
D. The Pyramid truck driver

10. Who does Bill the parakeet belong to?
A. Wayne Hoobler
B. Kilgore Trout
C. Mary Alice Miller
D. Harry LeSabre

11. What city does Trout visit before going to Midland City?
A. Boston
B. Chicago
C. Detroit
D. New York City

12. What is Harry LeSabre's secret?
A. He is in love with Dwayne
B. He wants to quit his job at the Pontiac agency
C. He is going insane
D. He is a transexual

13. **What is the motto of The Robo-Magic Corporation of America?**
    A. And so on
    B. Etc.
    C. Let Us Do Your Nigger Work!
    D. Goodbye, Blue Monday

14. **Whose wardrobe does Dwayne criticize?**
    A. Wayne Hoobler
    B. Francine Pefko
    C. Bunny Hoover
    D. Harry LeSabre

15. **What holiday is included in the timeframe of the story?**
    A. Easter
    B. Christmas
    C. Memorial Day
    D. Veteran's Day

16. **What does the narrator blame Dwayne Hoover's insanity on?**
    A. Sexual frustration
    B. Creative frustration
    C. Anger
    D. Bad chemicals

17. **What country is Cyprain Ukwende from?**
    A. America
    B. Nigeria
    C. Kenya
    D. South Africa

18. **What book turns Dwayne Hoover into a maniac?**
    A. "This Means You"
    B. "Now It Can Be Told"
    C. "Gilgongo!"
    D. "Plague on Wheels"

19. **What question does Trout read on the wall of the bathroom in the pornographic movie theater?**
    A. "Where am I?"
    B. "Why?"
    C. "Who are you?"
    D. "What is the purpose of life?"

20. **Who approaches Trout on Forty-Second Street?**
    A. Dwayne Hoover
    B. A madman
    C. Two black prostitutes
    D. The narrator

21. **Who is Trout's attack blamed on?**
    A. The Pluto Gang
    B. One of his characters
    C. The black prostitutes
    D. The manager of the movie theater

22. **Where does Dwayne sleep the night before his rampage?**
    A. In his car
    B. In his home
    C. The new Holiday Inn
    D. In the street

23. **What does it say on the side of the truck in which Trout hitches a ride?**
    A. Anchor
    B. Pyramid
    C. Fast
    D. Egypt

24. **Where does Dwayne Hoover first meet Wayne Hoobler?**
    A. In the kitchen of the new Holiday Inn
    B. Inside the Pontiac agnecy
    C. In the Pontiac agency parking lot
    D. On the street

25. **What is the name of Wayne Hoobler's imagined world?**
    A. Never Never Land
    B. Infinity
    C. Fairy Land
    D. Once Upon a Time Land

Quiz 1 Answer Key

1. **(B)** Science-fiction writer
2. **(A)** Business owner
3. **(C)** Lyle and Kyle Hoover
4. **(A)** Doodley-squat
5. **(D)** Pornographic literature
6. **(C)** Kilgore Trout
7. **(D)** Eliot Rosewater
8. **(D)** That he should be President
9. **(C)** Fred T. Barry
10. **(B)** Kilgore Trout
11. **(D)** New York City
12. **(D)** He is a transexual
13. **(D)** Goodbye, Blue Monday
14. **(D)** Harry LeSabre
15. **(D)** Veteran's Day
16. **(D)** Bad chemicals
17. **(B)** Nigeria
18. **(B)** "Now It Can Be Told"
19. **(D)** "What is the purpose of life?"
20. **(C)** Two black prostitutes
21. **(A)** The Pluto Gang
22. **(C)** The new Holiday Inn
23. **(B)** Pyramid
24. **(C)** In the Pontiac agency parking lot
25. **(C)** Fairy Land

Quiz 2

1. **Why is Wayne Hoobler at the Pontiac dealership?**
    - A. To kill Dwayne Hoover
    - B. He wants to work in the Holiday Inn kitchen
    - C. To get a job from Dwayne Hoover
    - D. To find his mother

2. **How many times has Trout been married?**
    - A. Once
    - B. Three
    - C. Twice
    - D. Never

3. **What did Trout's son, Leo, do?**
    - A. Died in Vietnam
    - B. Tried to kill his father
    - C. Joined the Viet Cong
    - D. Wrote a competitive story

4. **How does Dwayne tell Lyle and Kyle apart?**
    - A. Lyle wears overalls
    - B. Lyle has a broken nose
    - C. Kyle speaks with a lisp
    - D. Kyle wears a pork-pie hat

5. **What made the Bermuda Erns become extinct?**
    - A. The war
    - B. Athlete's foot
    - C. Mad Cow Disease
    - D. Poisonous gas

6. **What is destroying the Scared Miracle Cave?**
    - A. Maggots
    - B. Tourism
    - C. An infestation of squirrels
    - D. Polluted bubbles

7. **What was the name of the farm when Dwayne's stepfather bought it?**
    A. Bermuda Ern Farm
    B. Monday Farm
    C. Sacred Miracle Farm
    D. Bluebird Farm

8. **What state has been the most decimated by human development?**
    A. West Virginia
    B. Pennsylvania
    C. New York
    D. Ohio

9. **Who owns most of West Virigina?**
    A. Dwayne Hoover
    B. Eliot Rosewater
    C. The Pyramid truck driver
    D. The narrator

10. **Which of the following characters has never read anything by Kilgore Trout?**
    A. Dwayne Hoover
    B. Eliot Rosewater
    C. Beatrice Keedsler
    D. The Pyramid truck driver

11. **Who raped Patty Keene?**
    A. Don Breedlove
    B. Milo Maritimo
    C. Dwayne Hoover
    D. Bunny Hoover

12. **What machine are humans most compared to throughout the book?**
    A. Typewriters
    B. Vending Machines
    C. Cars
    D. Movie Reels

13. **What does Patty Keene want from Dwayne?**
    A. A big tip
    B. Sex
    C. Love advice
    D. Financial support

14. **How was George Hickman Bannister killed?**
    A. Suicide
    B. In a car accident
    C. In Viet Nam
    D. Playing football

15. **What does the sign on Francine's wall say?**
    A. Her name
    B. Don't Ask Me
    C. Nerve Center
    D. The Hub

16. **What is Francine's pact with Dwayne?**
    A. To have sex whenever he wants to
    B. To never say she loves him
    C. To never hire black people
    D. To kill him if he goes crazy

17. **How did Francine Pefko's husband die?**
    A. In Viet Nam
    B. He commited suicide by drinking Drano
    C. He was murdered by the Pluto Gang
    D. In his sleep at home

18. **What type of execution method do Dwayne and Francine discuss in bed?**
    A. Hanging
    B. Lethal Injection
    C. The Electric Chair
    D. Firing Squad

19. **What does Dwayne think Francine asks him for?**
    A. A back massage
    B. A Colonel Sanders Kentucky Fried Chicken franchise
    C. An engagement ring
    D. Money

20. **What is Harry and Grace LeSabre's codeword for black people?**
    A. Horses
    B. Beetles
    C. Reindeer
    D. Ants

21. **Where do Harry and Grace LeSabre move?**
    A. Atlanta
    B. Maui
    C. New York City
    D. Switzerland

22. **Who advises Dwayne to go to the arts festival?**
    A. Wayne Hoobler
    B. Kilgore Trout
    C. Francine Pefko
    D. Harry LeSabre

23. **Which of the following characters is happy?**
    A. Dwayne Hoover
    B. Kilgore Trout
    C. Andy Lieber
    D. Bunny Hoover

24. **Where does Bunny Hoover live?**
    A. In Sacred Miracle Cave
    B. Skid Row
    C. With his father, Dwayne
    D. The new Holiday Inn

25. **What does Bunny do while he plays the piano?**
    A. Meditates
    B. Cries
    C. Sings
    D. Masturbates

Quiz 2 Answer Key

1. **(C)** To get a job from Dwayne Hoover
2. **(B)** Three
3. **(C)** Joined the Viet Cong
4. **(B)** Lyle has a broken nose
5. **(B)** Athlete's foot
6. **(D)** Polluted bubbles
7. **(D)** Bluebird Farm
8. **(A)** West Virginia
9. **(B)** Eliot Rosewater
10. **(C)** Beatrice Keedsler
11. **(A)** Don Breedlove
12. **(C)** Cars
13. **(D)** Financial support
14. **(D)** Playing football
15. **(C)** Nerve Center
16. **(B)** To never say she loves him
17. **(A)** In Viet Nam
18. **(C)** The Electric Chair
19. **(B)** A Colonel Sanders Kentucky Fried Chicken franchise
20. **(C)** Reindeer
21. **(B)** Maui
22. **(C)** Francine Pefko
23. **(C)** Andy Lieber
24. **(B)** Skid Row
25. **(A)** Meditates

Quiz 3

1. **What were both the narrator's mother and Celia Hoover afraid of?**
   A. Their families
   B. Chemicals
   C. Having their photo taken
   D. Babies

2. **What is one thing Celia Hoover used to collect?**
   A. Pianos
   B. Tinkling music boxes
   C. Pictures
   D. Impressionist paintings

3. **What is the name of the dairy at the Adult Correctional Institution at Shpherdstown?**
   A. Queen of the Prairies
   B. Milk Duds
   C. Prison Milk
   D. Cows and Beef

4. **What is especially excellent at the Adult Correctional Institution at Shepherdstown?**
   A. The beds
   B. The coffee
   C. The health care in general
   D. The dental program

5. **What disease is the narrator pretty sure he has?**
   A. cancer
   B. schizophrenia
   C. HIV
   D. locomotor ataxia

6. **What does Bonnie MacMahon say every time she serves a martini?**
   A. "That'll be five dollars."
   B. "Here ya go."
   C. "Breakfast of Champions."
   D. "And for you?"

7. **Where did Beatrice Keedsler grow up?**
   A. England
   B. Midland City
   C. New York City
   D. France

8. **Which of the following words is NOT written on the side of one of the trucks drawn in this book?**
   A. Pyramid
   B. Zip
   C. Peerless Peerless
   D. Hertz

9. **What's blocking traffic on the Midland City stretch of the Interstate?**
   A. An accident between a Chevy and a Queen of the Prairies milk truck
   B. The artists arriving at the festival
   C. An alien invasion
   D. The Pyramid truck

10. **What does the narrator use for a symbol of time?**
    A. A serpent eating its tail
    B. A leak
    C. An hourglass
    D. A digital stopwatch

11. **How does the narrator divert the attention of Harold Newcomb Wilbur, the bartender?**
    A. He makes the telephone ring
    B. He takes off his sunglasses
    C. He starts a conversation
    D. He does a dance on the table

12. **What crime is Ned Lingamon in jail for?**
    A. Murdering a black man
    B. Escaping from jail the first time
    C. Trespassing
    D. Killing his own baby

13. **Which symbol does the narrator NOT draw on the tabletop with his finger?**
    A. An apple
    B. Pi
    C. Infinity
    D. Zero

14. **What is Rabo Karabekian's painting called?**
    A. The Dance of the Lions
    B. Roman Emperor
    C. The Temptation of Saint Anthony
    D. Midland City: The Asshole of the Universe

15. **Who feeds Wayne Hoobler?**
    A. Eldon Robbins
    B. Dwayne Hoover
    C. Francine Pefko
    D. Bonnie MacMahon

16. **What does Leroy Joyce do in the story Bonnie MacMahon tells?**
    A. Severs his own penis
    B. Kills Bonnie's husband
    C. Kills his jailor
    D. Jumps out of the electric chair

17. **What sport is Mary Alice Miller famous for?**
    A. Tennis
    B. Swimming
    C. Water Polo
    D. Basketball

18. **Who is the Queen of the Festival of the Arts?**
    A. Bonnie MacMahon
    B. Gloria Browning
    C. Mary Alice Miller
    D. Patty Keene

19. **Whose picture is on Mary Alice Miller's gold medal?**
    A. Saint Anthony
    B. Saint Sebastian
    C. Eliot Rosewater
    D. Saint Athanasius

20. **Where does the spiritual climax of the book occur?**
    A. In the cocktail lounge of the new Holiday Inn
    B. In the Pyramid Truck
    C. In the office of the Pontiac Agency
    D. In Sugar Creek

21. **Why does Bonnie MacMahon yell at Rabo Karabekian?**
    A. Because he laughed at her story about Leroy Joyce
    B. Because he refursed a martini
    C. Because he insulted Mary Alice Miller
    D. Because of his ugly sweatshirt

22. **What does the narrator think of Karabekian?**
    A. That he is a brilliant artist
    B. That he is a vain and weak and trashy man
    C. That his painting deserved to be bought for $50,000
    D. That he deserves to be attacked by Dwayne Hoover

23. **What does the dayglo tape on Karabekian's painting represent?**
    A. The environment
    B. Plant life
    C. Machinery
    D. Awareness

24. **Why are Trout's feet hot?**
    A. He is standing on hot asphalt
    B. His shoes are too tight
    C. They are artistic
    D. They are caked in plastic

25. **Who is polluting Sugar Creek?**
    A. The army
    B. Sacred Miracle Cave
    C. Bermuda Erns
    D. The Barrytron plant

Quiz 3 Answer Key

1. **(C)** Having their photo taken
2. **(B)** Tinkling music boxes
3. **(A)** Queen of the Prairies
4. **(D)** The dental program
5. **(B)** schizophrenia
6. **(C)** "Breakfast of Champions."
7. **(B)** Midland City
8. **(B)** Zip
9. **(A)** An accident between a Chevy and a Queen of the Prairies milk truck
10. **(A)** A serpent eating its tail
11. **(A)** He makes the telephone ring
12. **(D)** Killing his own baby
13. **(A)** An apple
14. **(C)** The Temptation of Saint Anthony
15. **(A)** Eldon Robbins
16. **(A)** Severs his own penis
17. **(B)** Swimming
18. **(C)** Mary Alice Miller
19. **(B)** Saint Sebastian
20. **(A)** In the cocktail lounge of the new Holiday Inn
21. **(C)** Because he insulted Mary Alice Miller
22. **(B)** That he is a vain and weak and trashy man
23. **(D)** Awareness
24. **(D)** They are caked in plastic
25. **(D)** The Barrytron plant

Quiz 4

1. **Who are the Maritimos?**
    A. A gangster family
    B. The owners of the new Holiday Inn
    C. Innocent bystanders of Dwayne's rampage
    D. A competing car dealership

2. **What does the narrator think is the proper ending for any story?**
    A. The end
    B. And so on
    C. And that was that
    D. Etc.

3. **What surrounds Trout when he enters the lobby of the new Holiday Inn?**
    A. Artists
    B. Mirrors
    C. Paintings
    D. Gangsters

4. **Why is Trout surprised by Milo Maritimo?**
    A. Because Milo knows who he is
    B. Because Milo is a homosexual
    C. Because Milo is a gangster
    D. Because he recognizes Milo as a former student

5. **What story of Trout's is Milo Maritimo currently reading?**
    A. The Smart Bunny
    B. Now It Can Be Told
    C. Plague on Wheels
    D. The Barring-gaffner of Bagnialto, or This Year's Masterpiece

6. **What is Dwayne Hoover mouthing to himself as he sits in the cocktail lounge?**
    A. "And so on"
    B. "Schizophrenia"
    C. "Drano"
    D. Goodbye, Blue Monday"

7. **What does NOT light up in the ultraviolet lights in the cocktail lounge?**
    A. Bunny Hoover's teeth
    B. Trout's shirt
    C. The narrator's shirt
    D. Bonnie MacMahon's uniform

8. **What letter does the narrator want to add to the equation E=mc^2?**
    A. M for Man
    B. A for Awareness
    C. L for Life
    D. S for Story

9. **Why does the narrator think northerners were frustrated by the Civil War?**
    A. Because they, too, were racist
    B. Because racism still exists
    C. Because they were cheated out of the "spoils:" slaves
    D. Because they wish the South had seceded

10. **How is the BLINC system related to Midland City?**
    A. It was built by Trout's company
    B. It was sold by the Pyramid truck driver
    C. Its nerve center originally was the brain of the I[Robo-Magic]
    D. It was invented by Eliot Rosewater's ancestors

11. **What does the narrator's bracelet say?**
    A. WO1 Jon Sparks 3-19-71
    B. W.W.J.D.?
    C. Awareness
    D. We are ALL machines

12. **Who finds the narrator's bracelet?**
    A. Wayne Hoobler
    B. Francine Pefko
    C. Don Miller
    D. Harry LeSabre

13. **From whom did the black people in Midland City learn to imitate birds?**
    A. Bonnie Keedsler
    B. Fred T. Barry
    C. Lottie Davis
    D. Fred T. Barry's mother

14. **What "extraordinarily unnatural" thing does the narrator have Dwayne do to make Trout uncomfortable?**
    A. Step on Trout's plastic-encased toes
    B. Give Trout a kiss
    C. Smack Trout across the face, twice
    D. Dig his chin into Trout's shoulder

15. **What is Don Miller doing during Dwayne's rampage?**
    A. Learning French
    B. Training Mary Alice Miller in swimming
    C. Practicing fencing
    D. Drinking a cocktail

16. **What does Abe Cohen, the jeweler, say about Mary Alice Miller?**
    A. "Hot dog!"
    B. "There she goes!"
    C. "Pure tuna fish!"
    D. "What a lady!"

17. **What does Bunny Hoover do when his father approaches him at the piano bar?**
    A. Stops playing immediately
    B. Defends himself
    C. Jumps up and hits Dwayne first
    D. Meditates

18. **Which of the following characters does Dwayne NOT injure?**
    A. Francine Pefko
    B. Bonnie MacMahon
    C. Mary Alice Miller
    D. Beatrice Keedsler

19. **What does Dwayne call out in the parking lot?**
   A. "Come out, come out, wherever you are"
   B. "Where am I?"
   C. "Olly-olly-ox-in-freeeeee"
   D. "Wayne Hoooooobler!"

20. **How did Martha Simmons die?**
   A. She overdosed on chemicals
   B. She was murdered
   C. She was bitten by a rabid bat while trying to rescue it
   D. She committed suicide by drinking Drano

21. **Which of the following characters has a live mother?**
   A. Wayne Hoobler
   B. Dwayne Hoover
   C. Eliot Rosewater
   D. None of the above

22. **How is the narrator injured during Dwayne's rampage?**
   A. He isn't
   B. He falls into Sugar Creek and is coated in plastic
   C. Somebody jumps backward and breaks his toe
   D. Dwayne socks him in the stomach

23. **What happens to Don Breedlove?**
   A. He becomes deaf
   B. He is raped
   C. He escapes from the rampage unscathed
   D. He is killed in the rampage

24. **What does Dr. Miasma refuse to help Cyprian Ukwende do inside the ambulance?**
   A. Amputate a black man's foot unnecessarily
   B. Find some shears to cut the plastic coating from Dwayne's shoes
   C. Hold down Dwayne Hoover
   D. Drive the vehicle

25. **Why does Kazak attack the narrator?**
   A. Because Kazak knows the narrator is the Creator of the Universe
   B. Because Kazak recognizes the narrator as his tormenter
   C. Because he is trained to be ferocious
   D. Because the narrator was taunting him

Quiz 4 Answer Key

1. **(A)** A gangster family
2. **(D)** Etc.
3. **(B)** Mirrors
4. **(A)** Because Milo knows who he is
5. **(A)** The Smart Bunny
6. **(D)** Goodbye, Blue Monday"
7. **(C)** The narrator's shirt
8. **(B)** A for Awareness
9. **(C)** Because they were cheated out of the "spoils:" slaves
10. **(C)** Its nerve center originally was the brain of the I[Robo-Magic]
11. **(A)** WO1 Jon Sparks 3-19-71
12. **(A)** Wayne Hoobler
13. **(D)** Fred T. Barry's mother
14. **(D)** Dig his chin into Trout's shoulder
15. **(A)** Learning French
16. **(C)** "Pure tuna fish!"
17. **(D)** Meditates
18. **(C)** Mary Alice Miller
19. **(C)** "Olly-olly-ox-in-freeeeee"
20. **(C)** She was bitten by a rabid bat while trying to rescue it
21. **(D)** None of the above
22. **(C)** Somebody jumps backward and breaks his toe
23. **(A)** He becomes deaf
24. **(B)** Find some shears to cut the plastic coating from Dwayne's shoes
25. **(C)** Because he is trained to be ferocious

ClassicNotes

GrAdeSaver™

Getting you the grade since 1999™

Other ClassicNotes from GradeSaver™

1984
Absalom, Absalom
Adam Bede
The Adventures of Augie
    March
The Adventures of
    Huckleberry Finn
The Adventures of Tom
    Sawyer
The Aeneid
Agamemnon
The Age of Innocence
The Alchemist (Jonson)
Alice in Wonderland
All My Sons
All Quiet on the Western
    Front
All the King's Men
All the Pretty Horses
The Ambassadors
American Beauty
Angela's Ashes
Animal Farm
Anna Karenina
Antigone
Antony and Cleopatra
Aristotle's Ethics
Aristotle's Poetics
Aristotle's Politics
As I Lay Dying
As You Like It
Astrophil and Stella
The Awakening
Babbitt
The Bacchae
Bartleby the Scrivener

The Bean Trees
The Bell Jar
Beloved
Benito Cereno
Beowulf
Bhagavad-Gita
Billy Budd
Black Boy
Bleak House
Bless Me, Ultima
The Bloody Chamber
Bluest Eye
The Bonfire of the
    Vanities
The Book of the Duchess
    and Other Poems
Brave New World
Breakfast at Tiffany's
Breakfast of Champions
The Brothers Karamazov
The Burning Plain and
    Other Stories
A Burnt-Out Case
By Night in Chile
Call of the Wild
Candide
The Canterbury Tales
Cat on a Hot Tin Roof
Cat's Cradle
Catch-22
The Catcher in the Rye
The Caucasian Chalk
    Circle
The Cherry Orchard
The Chocolate War
The Chosen

A Christmas Carol
Chronicle of a Death
    Foretold
Civil Disobedience
Civilization and Its
    Discontents
A Clockwork Orange
The Color of Water
The Color Purple
Comedy of Errors
Communist Manifesto
A Confederacy of
    Dunces
Confessions
Connecticut Yankee in
    King Arthur's Court
The Consolation of
    Philosophy
Coriolanus
The Count of Monte
    Cristo
Crime and Punishment
The Crucible
Cry, the Beloved
    Country
The Crying of Lot 49
Cymbeline
Daisy Miller
Death in Venice
Death of a Salesman
The Death of Ivan Ilych
Democracy in America
Devil in a Blue Dress
Dharma Bums
The Diary of a Young
    Girl by Anne Frank

For our full list of over 250 Study Guides, Quizzes,
Sample College Application Essays, Literature Essays and E-texts, visit:

www.gradesaver.com

ClassicNotes

GrAdeSaver™

Getting you the grade since 1999™

Other ClassicNotes from GradeSaver™

Manhattan Transfer
Mansfield Park
MAUS
The Mayor of
    Casterbridge
Measure for Measure
Medea
Merchant of Venice
Metamorphoses
The Metamorphosis
Middlemarch
Midsummer Night's
    Dream
Moby Dick
Moll Flanders
Mother Courage and Her
    Children
Mrs. Dalloway
Much Ado About
    Nothing
My Antonia
Mythology
Native Son
Night
Nine Stories
No Exit
Notes from Underground
O Pioneers
The Odyssey
Oedipus Rex or Oedipus
    the King
Of Mice and Men
The Old Man and the Sea
On Liberty
On the Road

One Day in the Life of
    Ivan Denisovich
One Flew Over the
    Cuckoo's Nest
One Hundred Years of
    Solitude
Oroonoko
Othello
Our Town
Pale Fire
Paradise Lost
A Passage to India
The Pearl
Persuasion
Phaedra
Phaedrus
The Picture of Dorian
    Gray
Poems of W.B. Yeats:
    The Rose
Poems of W.B. Yeats:
    The Tower
The Poisonwood Bible
Portrait of the Artist as a
    Young Man
Pride and Prejudice
The Prince
Prometheus Bound
Pudd'nhead Wilson
Pygmalion
Rabbit, Run
A Raisin in the Sun
The Real Life of
    Sebastian Knight
The Red Badge of
    Courage

The Remains of the Day
The Republic
Rhinoceros
Richard II
Richard III
The Rime of the Ancient
    Mariner
Robinson Crusoe
Roll of Thunder, Hear
    My Cry
Romeo and Juliet
A Room of One's Own
A Room With a View
Rosencrantz and
    Guildenstern Are
    Dead
Salome
The Scarlet Letter
The Scarlet Pimpernel
The Secret Life of Bees
Secret Sharer
Sense and Sensibility
A Separate Peace
Shakespeare's Sonnets
Shantaram
Siddhartha
Silas Marner
Sir Gawain and the
    Green Knight
Sister Carrie
Six Characters in Search
    of an Author
Slaughterhouse Five
Snow Falling on Cedars
The Social Contract

For our full list of over 250 Study Guides, Quizzes,
Sample College Application Essays, Literature Essays and E-texts, visit:

www.gradesaver.com